Walter Robson

Britain
1750 - 1900

Sch

OXFORD
UNIVERSITY PRESS

OXFORD
UNIVERSITY PRESS

Great Clarendon Street, Oxford OX2 6DP
Oxford University Press is a department of the University of Oxford.
It furthers the University's objective of excellence in research, scholarship,
and education by publishing worldwide in

Oxford New York
Auckland Cape Town Dar es Salaam Hong Kong Karachi
Kuala Lumpur Madrid Melbourne Mexico City Nairobi
New Delhi Shanghai Taipei Toronto

With offices in
Argentina Austria Brazil Chile Czech Republic France Greece
Guatemala Hungary Italy Japan South Korea Poland Portugal
Singapore Switzerland Thailand Turkey Ukraine Vietnam

Oxford is a registered trade mark of Oxford University Press
in the UK and in certain other countries

© Oxford University Press 1993

The moral rights of the author have been asserted

Database right Oxford University Press (maker)

First published 1993

ISBN : 978 0 19 8335436

15 14

Typeset by MS Filmsetting Limited, Frome, Somerset
Printed in Singapore by KHL Printing Co Pte Ltd

Acknowledgements

Page 4 British Library; p5 Cambridge University/Crown Copyright; p6tr & cr Museum of English Rural Life, Reading; p7 British Library; p8c Illustrated London News, b British Library; p9 Bridgeman/Victoria & Albert Museum, London; p10cl Bridgeman Art Library, br British Library; p12–13t Mansell Collection, p13b Metropolitan Museum, New York; p15t E.T. Archive/Ironbridge Gorge Museum, b & p16 Mary Evans Picture Library; p17 Science Museum, London; p18 National Museums & Galleries on Merseyside (Walker Art Gallery); p19 Bridgeman; p20–21b Manchester City Art Gallery, p21t British Library; p22 Mansell Collection; p24 Bridgeman/Ackeman & Johnson Ltd, London; p25t Mansell Collection, b British Waterways; p26 & p28 British Library; p29t Bridgeman/ Museum of British Transport, p29b & p30 Bridgeman/ Science Museum; p31 Mansell Collection; p32c Mary Evans, bl Charles D. Cobb/National Maritime Museum, London; p33 Mary Evans; p34t & b Mansell Collection; p35 Bridgeman/Giraudon; p36cl & br British Museum; p36–37t Mansell Collection; p39 Sir John Soane's Museum; p40–41 British Museum; p42 Hulton Deutsch Collection; pp43, 44, 46 Mansell Collection; p47t British Museum, b Illustrated London News; p48t Bridgeman/Guildhall Library London, b Mansell Collection; p49 British Library; p51c Mansell Collection, b Hulton Deutsch Collection; p52 Mary Evans; p55 Mansell Collection; p56 Illustrated London News; pp57 & 58t & b Victoria & Albert Museum; pp59 & 60tr Mary Evans; p60tl Punch, b Hulton Deutsch; p61 E.T./ Bibliotèque des Arts Décoratifs, Paris; p62b Mary Evans; p64 E.T. Archive; p65 & 66t Mansell Collection, p66b E.T. Archive; p68t Mansell Collection, b Bridgeman Art Library; p69t & b National Gallery of Ireland, Dublin; pp70, 71, 72 Mansell Collection; p73 Hulton Deutsch; p74 Bridgeman/British Library; p76t British Library, b Mansell Collection; p78t E.T./National Maritime Museum, b Royal Geographical Society, London; p79 British Museum; p80 & 81 Hulton Deutsch; p82 Mansell Collection; p83 Hulton Deutsch; p84 National Trust; p85t Mansell Collection, c Brighton Borough Council, b Museum of London; p86tr Bridgeman/Wallington Hall, bl Tate Gallery, London; pp89 & 90 Mansell Collection; p91 British Museum; p92t Punch, b E.T. Archive; p93 National Portrait Gallery, London; p94 Mansell Collection.

Cover: Science Museum, London.

Illustrations by Juliet Breese, John James, Peter Kent, Martin Sanders, and Duncan Storr.

Contents

Preface

The title of this series is *Access to History*, and accessibility is its keynote – accessibility to National Curriculum History, in terms of both the Programme of Study and the Attainment Target.

The exercises, which refer to the text, sources, and illustrations, are intended to extend factual knowledge, promote comprehension, and develop a range of skills, all consistent with the revised National Curriculum requirements for knowledge, skills and understanding. The "criteria grid" (at the end of the book) shows how the individual exercises relate to these requirements.

It is not expected that pupils will work through the book unaided. Teachers will wish to omit some exercises and amend others. They will probably decide that some exercises which are set for individual work would be tackled more successfully by using a group or class approach, with the teacher him/herself as leader. The book's aim is to provide teachers with a useful set of resources, not to usurp their role.

The exercises with the fill-in blanks may be either photocopied to provide answer sheets and homework assignments or copied out by the pupils and filled in as they go along.

Agriculture, 1750-1870

A Squires and labourers

Britain was still a country of villages and farms in 1750. Far more people worked on the land than in any other trade. The landowners were the leading men. Some of them were great lords, with big estates and country houses. The **squires** (or **gentry**), owned less land than the lords. But the squires (see **Source 1a**) were still the top men in their villages.

Tenant farmers rented land from the lords or squires. Most of them employed **labourers** to work their fields. Some of these workers (the young, unmarried men and women) lived in the farmers' homes and worked full-time. The rest were employed by the farmers only at busy times of the year. They lived with their families in rough cottages, and had a hard life.

In 1750 many villages in England still had three or four **open fields**, divided into strips. Even more still had some **common land**. But open fields and common land were disappearing. **Enclosures** were eating them up, turning them into smaller fields, with hedges or fences round them. By 1830, there were hardly any open fields left.

Enclosures meant more money for landowners and tenant farmers. They were not so good for labourers, though. They lost the right to use the common land. That was where they had kept their cows and sheep. And money from selling butter, cheese, and wool had kept hunger from their doors. On the other hand, enclosures meant work and wages. Landlords and tenants needed labour to make fences, dig ditches, and till the fields.

Now try Exercises 1.1 and 1.2.

Source 1a

A poacher is brought before the squire. (The squire is both landlord and Justice of the Peace.) Poaching was a serious crime, and the punishment could be seven years' transportation. That is why the poacher's wife and child are on their knees.

Exercise 1.1

Read **Section A** and look at **Source 1a**. Copy the sentences and fill in the blanks.

a Great lords and squires owned _____ .

b Many squires were _____ of the Peace.

c Tenant farmers had to pay _____ to their landlords.

d Young, _____ farm workers often lived in the farmer's house.

e _____ meant turning open fields and common land into smaller, separate fields.

f By _____ hardly any villages still had open fields.

g Labourers lost the right to keep animals on the _____ land.

h Enclosures usually meant extra _____ and _____ for labourers.

Source 1b

A few days ago, a group of women were arrested for breaking down the fences that enclosed a common. The magistrates at Burton ordered them to be put in Stafford Jail. But the people heard what was going on, and gathered along the road. They attacked the guards with stones and lumps of soil, rescued the women, and led them off in triumph.

Adapted from the *Northampton Mercury* newspaper, 10 June 1771.

Source 1c

A million acres of land have been enclosed in the last 30 or 40 years. Most of it was open-fields before enclosure. The land used to grow crops worth 30 shillings [£1.50] an acre. Now it grows crops worth £3 an acre. So enclosing this land has brought in at least £1,500,000 more a year.

Adapted from an article written by Arthur Young in 1790.

Exercise 1.2

Read **Sources 1b** and **1c**, then answer the questions in sentences.

a Why was Arthur Young (**Source 1c**) in favour of enclosures?

b Who got the extra money that came from farming enclosed land?

c Which group of people did Arthur Young not think about?

d Why were the women in **Source 1b** sent to Stafford Jail?

e Why do you think the women broke down the fences?

f What does **Source 1b** tell us about the feelings of the common people?

B Improved farming methods

Enclosures made more money for land-lords and tenants. Landlords laid new drains, to make wet land drier, and put up new farm buildings. Then they urged their tenants to try new farming methods. The tenants made bigger profits, and the landlords put up the rents.

Enclosed fields. You can still see the Medieval strips in some of the fields.

On enclosed land, farmers made up their own minds which crops to grow, when to sow the seed, when to harvest the crop, etc. (They did not have to go along with the rest of the village.) This meant that they could try out new crops, such as turnips and clover. And farmers who grew clover found that they did not need to leave the land fallow every third year. (Look at the chart 'Crop Rotation'.)

Turnips and clover were winter food for cattle and sheep. Farmers who grew them did not need to kill off most of their animals in the autumn. And after enclosures, farmers kept their own cattle in their own fields — they did not have to mix with the others on the common. So careful farmers could be sure that their animals were kept free from disease.

For some, farming became a science. **Robert Bakewell** and the **Colling** brothers bred new kinds of sheep and cattle. They were bigger than other animals, gave more meat, and brought more profit to the farmer.

News of the farming changes was spread in books and papers. Great lords, and King George III himself, laid out 'model farms' to show what could be done. But not all landlords and farmers were quick to change. Most farmers did not start growing turnips and clover until after 1800.

Now try Exercises 1.3 and 1.4.

Selective breeding led to an increase in the size of cattle and sheep

Before

After

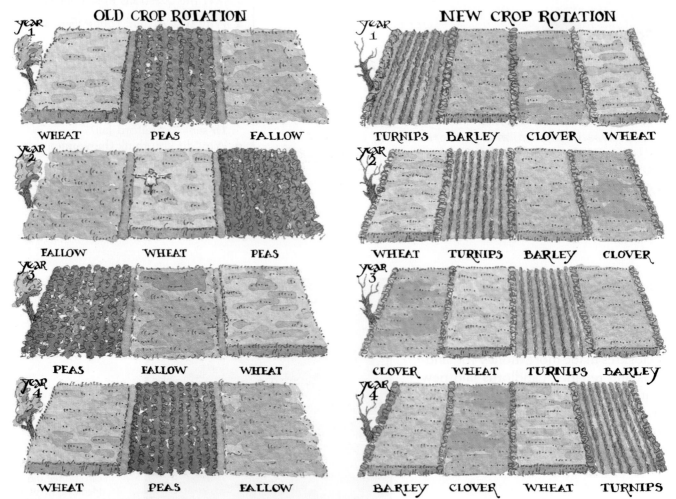

OLD CROP ROTATION

year 1: WHEAT — PEAS — FALLOW
year 2: FALLOW — WHEAT — PEAS
year 3: PEAS — FALLOW — WHEAT
year 4: WHEAT — PEAS — FALLOW

NEW CROP ROTATION

year 1: TURNIPS — BARLEY — CLOVER — WHEAT
year 2: WHEAT — TURNIPS — BARLEY — CLOVER
year 3: CLOVER — WHEAT — TURNIPS — BARLEY
year 4: BARLEY — CLOVER — WHEAT — TURNIPS

Farmers found that clover put nitrogen back into the soil, so there was no need to leave it to rest (lie fallow) every third or fourth year.

This four Wheel Drill Plow, with a Seed and a Manure Hopper, was first Invented in the Year 1745. and is now in Use with W.ᵐ Ellis at Little Gaddesden near Hempstead in Hertfordshire. where any person may View the same. It is so light that a Man may Draw it, but Generally drawn by a pony or little Horse.

Source 1d

After the land had been enclosed, go-ahead farmers used machines like this seed drill on their land

Source 1e

I have just seen one of the new seed-drills. It is strong, but not heavy, has two wheels, and is drawn by one or two horses. It makes three furrows at a time, sows seed into them, then covers the seed with soil. It does the work much more quickly and exactly than it can be done by hand.

Adapted from the *Leeds Intelligencer* newspaper, 5 June 1764.

Fact and opinion

Facts are things that are true, or were true in the past. An event that happened is a fact. Things that you can see, or touch, or hear are facts. These are facts: the women in **Source 1b** broke down some fences; the local people rescued the women.

An **opinion** is what someone thinks, believes, or feels. It tells us about a person's likes and dislikes, and whether he or she thinks things are good or bad. This is an opinion: the magistrates in **Source 1b** thought that the women were criminals.

Exercise 1.3

Read **Section B** and **Source 1e**, and study **Source 1d**.

a In what ways is the seed-drill described in **Source 1e** the same as the drill shown in **Source 1d**? In what ways are the two drills different? (Write a paragraph).
b Either copy **Source 1d** or draw a picture of the seed-drill described in **Source 1e**.

Source 1f

A hundred years ago, the potato was thought to be a food fit only for the poorest of the poor. Now it is eaten by rich and poor alike. But it is the poor who have gained most – it has given them a better standard of life and saved them from the famine. It can be roasted, boiled, fried, chopped up, or mixed with bacon, or onions, or flour.

Adapted from a book written by Sir Frederick Eden in 1797.

Exercise 1.4

Read the note on '**Fact and Opinion**', and read **Source 1f**.

a Write down as many facts as you can find about potatoes in **Source 1f**.
b What were rich people's opinions about potatoes **i** in 1697, and **ii** in 1797?
c Why did the author of **Source 1f** have a good opinion of potatoes?

7

C Good times and bad

The years after 1750 were a time of high profits for farmers and good rents for landlords. The best years were from 1793 to 1815, when Britain was at war with France, and food prices were very high. It was a time of **boom** in farming.

When peace came in 1815, food prices, profits, and rents fell. The years 1815 to 1830 were a time of **slump** for farmers and their landlords. Some tenants gave up the struggle and became labourers. Others left the land, and looked for work in the growing towns. Labourers' wages were always low, but in times of slump they fell even lower. In the south of England in 1830 they sank to 10 shillings (50p) a week.

From about 1835, though, food prices rose again. And between 1850 and 1870 farmers and landowners enjoyed another boom. They spent money to improve the land, on drainage pipes and steam pumps, and on new fertilizers. They bought new machines such as binders and reapers, and steam-driven threshers. Even the labourers shared in the boom – in good times the farmers could afford to pay them a decent wage.

Now try Exercise 1.5.

Farm labourers at work without machinery

Source **1g**

A steam-driven threshing machine – to separate the ears of grain from the straw

Exercise 1.5

Read **Section C**, and look at **Source 1g**.
Find words in **Section C** to fit the phrases below:

a Money to spare after the farmer had paid all his bills.
b A time of high prices and good profits.
c A time of low prices, low profits (or none at all), and low wages.
d Chemicals that farmers put on the land to make it more fertile.
e A horse-drawn machine to cut hay or corn.
f A steam-driven machine to separate the ears of grain from the straw.

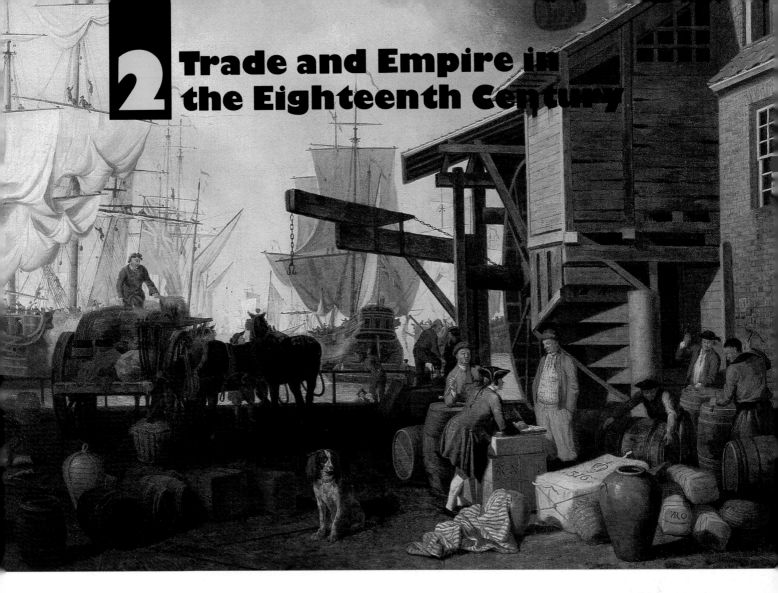

2 Trade and Empire in the Eighteenth Century

Goods being unloaded at the London customs house in the eighteenth century. A painting by Samuel Scott.

A Eighteenth-century trade

By 1750 Britain was the world's leading trading nation. Ships full of Swedish iron and China tea queued up to enter the ports. Cartloads of West Indian sugar and American tobacco rattled along the quays. Store-houses were packed with spices and rich cloths from India and the East.

Trade was growing all the time. In 1800, six times as much sugar reached Britain as in 1700. The ports were growing too — Bristol was twice as big in 1750 as in 1700. The merchants who owned the ships grew rich, bought land, and turned themselves into country squires.

Imports had to be paid for with **exports**. In 1750, Britain still sold her own woollen cloth to all parts of Europe. As well as cloth, though, she sold in Europe some of the spices and sugar that her merchants had brought from abroad. Each deal meant a handsome profit, of course.

Merchants also made big profits from the shameful trade in **slaves.** They bought slaves on the coast of West Africa, shipped them like cattle to the West Indies and America, and sold them to work cutting sugar-cane or picking tobacco and cotton. Then they brought home cargoes of sugar and tobacco to Britain.

Now try Exercise 2.1.

Exercise 2.1

Study **Section A.**
British merchants in the eighteenth century bought and sold iron, spices, tea, sugar, tobacco, woollen cloth, and slaves.
In which countries did they buy them, and where did they sell them?
Make a chart with columns headed 'Goods' (iron, spices, etc.), 'Where Bought' and 'Where Sold'.

The Taj Mahal – built by the Mughal emperor Shah Jahan

B India

India's ruler was the **Mughal** emperor in Delhi. But the men with real power were the **princes** — the nawabs and rajahs who ruled the districts. They were just like kings, with their palaces, grand clothes, and hundreds of servants. Each prince had his army – men, horses, guns, and elephants.

India's wealth (in gems, perfumes, pepper, and fine cloth) attracted traders from Europe. And the Mughals allowed them to open 'factories', or trading posts, at places round the coast. (Look at the **Map.**)

By 1750, the British and French were the main westerners in India. They often quarrelled with each other, and took opposite sides in the wars among the nawabs and rajahs. In 1757 the British came out on top. They beat the French, and made themselves masters of Bengal. **Robert Clive** won his vital battle, at **Plassey**, by bribing an Indian prince not to fight.

The British in India were employed by the **East India Company**, a trading firm. Even the soldiers were paid by the company. After 1750, though, the

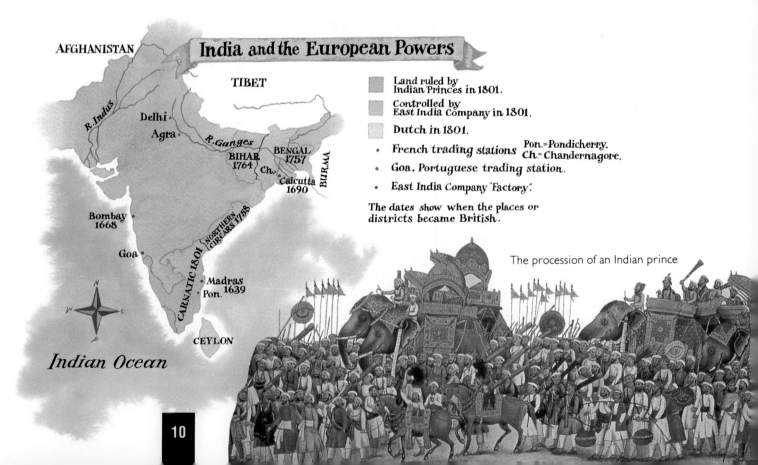

India and the European Powers

AFGHANISTAN

TIBET

R. Indus

Delhi
Agra

R. Ganges

BENGAL 1757
BIHAR 1764
Ch.
Calcutta 1690

BURMA

Bombay 1668

CARNATIC 1801 NORTHERN CIRCARS 1758

Goa

Madras 1639
Pon.

CEYLON

Indian Ocean

Land ruled by Indian Princes in 1801.

Controlled by East India Company in 1801.

Dutch in 1801.

• French trading stations Pon.=Pondicherry. Ch.=Chandernagore.

• Goa. Portuguese trading station.

• East India Company "Factory".

The dates show when the places or districts became British.

The procession of an Indian prince

company dealt with more than just trade. It began to take control of India. One by one, the princes agreed to accept British 'protection'. (The **Map** shows the spread of British rule.)

In the parts which they ruled, the British collected taxes, ran law courts, and kept law and order. They said that their rule was honest and fair, and better than India had known before. In fact, most of the East India Company's men cheated and took bribes. Those who lived long enough to come home brought big fortunes with them.

Now try Exercises 2.2 and 2.3.

Exercise 2.2

Read **Section B**, and study the **Map**. Find out when the following places or districts became British:

Carnatic, Madras, Northern Circars, Bombay, Calcutta, Bengal, Bihar.

Write out the names and dates in the correct order (earliest first).

Source 2a

The nawab of Bengal was a cruel and wicked tyrant. In 1756 he picked a quarrel with the English, and captured their base at Calcutta. He told his guards to put all the English prisoners into a dungeon called the 'Black Hole'. No less than 146 persons were locked into this small, airless space for a night. Next morning, only 23 of them were left alive.

Adapted from a book written by an Englishman, Sir Charles Oman, in 1895.

Source 2b

The story of the Black Hole of Calcutta may not be true. Most historians now think that an Englishman called Holwell made it up. (He wanted to make the British hate the nawab of Bengal.) No-one else who lived at that time mentioned it. Clive says nothing about it in his letters. After the war, the British did not make the nawab pay money to the victims' families.

Adapted from a book written by D. P. Singhal, an Indian historian, in 1983.

Historians sometimes disagree

Writers do not always say the same things about the people or events of the past. Here are some reasons why this may happen.
  i Writers who were present when events happened might know more than writers who have only used other books.
  ii As time has passed, some sources have been lost or destroyed.
  iii As time has passed, new sources have been discovered.
  iv Some historians have not bothered to read or look at all the sources.
  v Some authors take the side of their own country.

Exercise 2.3

Read the note 'Historians Sometimes Disagree' and **Sources 2a** and **2b**. Write out the sentences, and write either TRUE or FALSE after each of them. 'Oman' was the author of **Source 2a**. 'Singhal' was the author of **Source 2b**.

a Oman thought that the story of the 'Black Hole of Calcutta' was true.
b Oman may have talked to people who survived the 'Black Hole of Calcutta'.
c Oman must have read all the sources.
d If events happened as Oman described, Englishmen living in India at that time would have talked and written about them.
e Singhal also believed the 'Black Hole' story.
f Singhal had probably read more sources than Oman.
g **Source 2a** was written by an Englishman, and **Source 2b** by an Indian.

C The loss of the American colonies

Most of the east coast of North America was British in 1750. From the farmers and fishermen in the north to the tobacco-growers in the south, they all flew the British flag and obeyed British laws. (Look at the **Map**.)

Canada was French, and the French were often at war with Britain. In some parts of the British colonies, the men always had to be ready to defend their homes. So they were glad to have British troops on their side. And they paid taxes to help pay for the troops.

In 1763, after victory in war, Britain took Canada from France. So the threat to the colonies was gone. But the taxes remained. And it was **Parliament** in London that fixed the taxes and made the laws.

The laws on trade said that Americans must buy imports (e.g. tea) from British merchants. And they said that

exports (e.g. tobacco) must be sold to British merchants. In the colonies, they said that this was unfair. They said that they should fix their own taxes, and make their own laws.

The quarrel turned to war in 1775. The American 'rebels' formed an army and chose **George Washington** as their leader. At first, the army was badly armed and clothed. It nearly lost the war. Then the French sent help, and the tide began to turn. In 1781, the British army at **Yorktown** had to surrender to the French and the 'rebels'.

Peace was made in 1783. The colonies got their freedom, and joined together to form the **United States of America**. Britain kept Canada, though, and some loyal subjects moved there from the new U.S.A.

Now try Exercise 2.4.

The Boston Tea Party

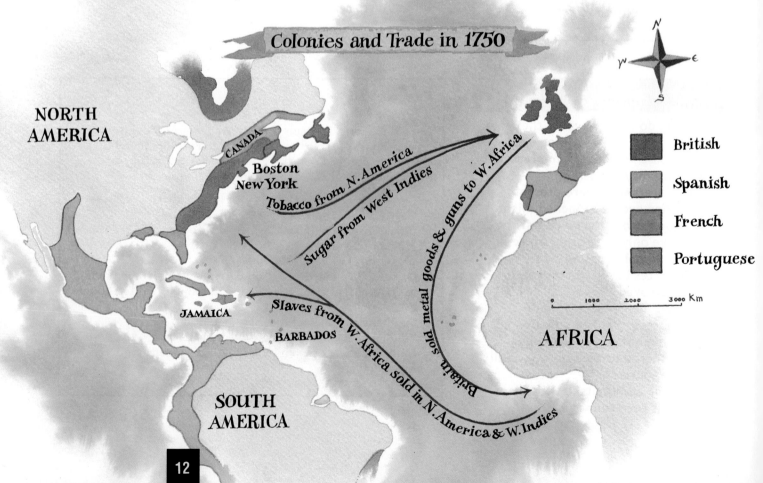

Colonies and Trade in 1750

NORTH AMERICA

CANADA

Boston
New York

Tobacco from N. America

Sugar from West Indies

Britain sold metal goods & guns to W. Africa

Slaves from W. Africa sold in N. America & W. Indies

JAMAICA

BARBADOS

SOUTH AMERICA

AFRICA

British
Spanish
French
Portuguese

0 1000 2000 3000 Km

Exercise 2.4

Read **Section C** and **Source 2e** and
study **Source 2d**.
Make notes for an essay on 'Sources
about the Boston Tea Party'.

a Which things can you learn from
   both sources?
b Which things can you learn from
   Source 2d only?
c Which things can you learn from
   Source 2e only?
d In what ways are picture sources **i**
   more useful and **ii** less useful than
   written sources?

Source 2e

*A law passed in 1773 said that
only the East India Company
could sell tea in America. The
Americans hated this law. They
said that they should be free to
buy tea from anyone. One
night in December 1773, a
band of men dressed as
Mohawk Indians climbed
aboard three ships in Boston
harbour. They found the
cargoes of tea, and tipped them
into the sea. This was the
famous 'Boston Tea Party'.
Soon after, the British passed a
law saying that the port of
Boston was closed until the tea
was paid for.*

Adapted from a book published by
the United States government in
1953.

George Washington

3 The Industrial Revolution – Iron, Steam and Coal

A The Industrial Revolution

Between 1750 and 1900 Britain went through a huge change in how and where men and women worked and lived. Students of history call it the **Industrial Revolution**.

In a few trades at first, people started to make things with **machines**, instead of by hand. The machines were in **mills** and **factories**, so men and women (and children) worked there, not in workshops or in their homes. Before long,

power (first water, then steam) was used to drive the machines.

Farming ceased to be the main work of the people. Its place was taken by industry. And as the mills and factories were mainly in **towns**, that is where people had to live. And finally, the **population** rose – in 1900 it was six times as large as 150 years before.

Now try Exercise 3.1.

Exercise 3.1

Read **Section A**, then copy out the chart, filling in the blank spaces.

Before Industrial Revolution	During and after Industrial Revolution
a Craftsmen made articles by hand.	In many trades, goods were made by _____ .
b Craftsmen worked at home or _____ .	Men, women, and children worked in _____ or _____ .
c Craftsmen used their own skill and strength.	Machines were driven by power (_____ or _____).
d _____ was most people's occupation.	Industry employed more and more people.
e Most people lived in _____ districts.	Far more people lived in _____ .

B The iron industry

Iron ore has to be heated (or **smelted**) to extract the iron. Until after 1700, the fuel for smelting was **charcoal** (partly burnt wood). But the demand for charcoal was eating up England's forests. And the iron industry could not grow if there was not enough fuel. (The sulphur in coal had a bad effect on iron, so coal could not be used for smelting.)

In 1709, though, **Abraham Darby** of Coalbrookdale in Shropshire discovered that if you first made coal into **coke** it could be used for smelting. The invention was kept secret for 30 years. Even then, the news spread slowly. It was the 1760s before coke was widely used.

Darby's methods produced good **cast iron**, which was used for guns and pots and pans. But they were no use for **wrought iron**, to make plough shares, tools, and nails. It was **Henry Cort** in 1784, with his 'puddling process', who found a way of using coke to make wrought iron.

Source 3a

Mr. Crawshay's iron works (at Merthyr Tydfil) are now the largest in Britain. The biggest thing there is the great water wheel. It is fifty feet across, and it has the power of fifty horses. There are six smelting furnaces, and around them are the forges and rolling mills. Forty years ago, this place was just a village. Now it is the largest town in Wales.

Adapted from a book written by Benjamin Malkin in 1804.

The first iron bridge, built at Coalbrookdale by Abraham Darby's firm in 1779

Source 3b

Iron works at Coalbrookdale in Shropshire in 1788

The work of Darby and Cort made iron cheap and plentiful. Big iron works were set up in South Wales, Scotland, the Midlands, and Yorkshire. By 1815 Britain turned out nearly ten times as much iron as in 1750.

The years 1750–1850 were the age of iron. It was used for beams in buildings, bridges, gas-pipes, and above all for machines. By the 1840s iron trains ran on iron tracks up and down the length of Britain. Iron was the key to the Industrial Revolution.

Now try Exercise 3.2.

Exercise 3.2

Read **Section B** and **Source 3a**, and look at **Source 3b**. Answer the questions.

a Who owned the iron works at Merthyr Tydfil?
b How do you know that the Merthyr Tydfil iron works used water power?
c What fuel do you think they used in the Merthyr Tydfil furnaces?
d About when did Merthyr Tydfil begin to grow into a town?
e How do you know that the Coalbrookdale iron works used water power?
f How do you know that the Coalbrookdale iron works used coke or coal?
g How many workers do you think that the Coalbrookdale iron works employed — under 20, between 20 and 100, over 100?

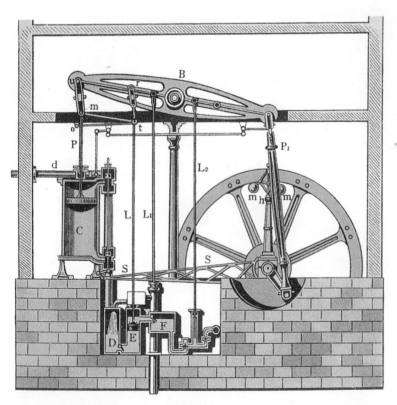

The steam engine designed by James Watt

C Steam engines

The most important of the iron machines was the steam engine. The looms and spindles of the mills were driven by steam. Steam engines pumped water from the mines, and hauled out men and coal. Railway trains were drawn by steam engines on wheels.

From 1700, steam engines were used to pump water out of mines. But they were slow and used a lot of coal. In the 1770s and 1780s, **James Watt**, a Scotsman, invented a much better engine. It needed less coal, and it could do more than just work a pump. Watt's engine could also turn a wheel, which meant that it could drive machines.

Watt's engines were made in Birmingham at **Matthew Boulton's** workshop. They were made one at a time at first — there were not enough skilled engineers to make the parts for more. By 1800 a few hundred were in use, in mines, cotton mills, and iron works.

The spread of steam power took place mainly after 1800. As more factories were built, more steam engines were needed. More workmen became skilled in making boilers and pistons. New firms followed Boulton's lead, supplying engines to all parts of Britain and selling them abroad.

Now try Exercise 3.3.

Source 3d

i The steam engine was used in a wide range of industries. Before the railway age, though, it was important only in cotton, iron, and mining.
ii Costs fell in British industry, and this made it easier to sell British goods abroad.

Adapted from a book written by Miss Phyllis Deane in 1965. The 'railway age' began in 1825.

Source 3c

Steam engines built 40 years ago are still in use. How many horses would have been worn out doing the same amount of work? How much corn would they have eaten? Steam engines use coal, so they give work to miners. And they help to mine the coal – draining water from the pits, and hauling up the coal. They drive engines in cotton mills and iron-works, and on railways. They are cheap to run, so the goods which they help to make are cheap. Because of this, we sell more abroad, and we are all better off.

Adapted from a book written by Andrew Ure in 1835.

Exercise 3.3

Read **Section C** and **Sources 3c** and **3d**.

a In a group, discuss what, if anything, the two sources say about
  i horses,
  ii which industries used steam engines,
  iii exports.

b Make a group display (with drawings and written work) showing the links between steam engines and i horses, ii industry, and iii exports.

Two Davy lamps. The fine mesh round the flame stopped the methane gas in the mine from exploding.

D Coal-mining

Ironworks and steam engines needed coal. As they spread, the demand for coal grew. So more mines were opened, and deeper shafts were sunk. Deeper pits meant more danger for the miners, above all from water and gas. An explosion at Felling pit on Tyneside in 1812 killed 92 men and boys.

Inventors tackled the problems, but only partly solved them. The steam engine helped with the pumping. Using two or more shafts produced a flow of air and better ventilation. **Sir Humphry Davy's** safety lamp (invented in 1815) reduced the risk from gas.

In Scotland the mine-owners employed women and girls as well as men and boys. (Their wages were lower than men's.) Inspectors in the 1830s found pits where boys and girls of four or five sat for hours in the dark, opening and closing trap-doors. Their report shocked the public. In 1842 Parliament passed a law which said that girls, women, and boys under ten could not work underground.

Now try Exercise 3.4.

Causes and Results

Causes come **before** results. Causes are the answer to the questions: **Why** did it happen? **Why** was it like that?
Results comes **after** causes.
We may say: 'Because of Cort's inventions, iron became cheap and popular.' In that case, 'Cort's inventions' is the **cause** and 'iron became cheap and popular' is the **result**.

A pithead with steam winding gear in about 1820

Exercise 3.4

Read **Section D** and the note on 'Causes and Results'. Then make notes on:

a The causes of **i** deeper mines being sunk, and **ii** some mine-owners employing women and children.
b The results of **i** mines becoming deeper, and **ii** inspectors going down mines in the 1830s.

4 The Industrial Revolution – Textiles

A From cottage to mill

Since the Middle Ages, making **woollen** cloth had been England's main industry. Most of the work was done by country people in their own homes. Labourers' wives would spin and weave when they had time to spare. Their husbands helped when there was no work for them on the farm.

Rich **clothiers** bought the raw wool, employed the spinners and weavers, and sold the finished cloth. Most of the time, they could sell all the cloth that was made. So they were glad when inventors came up with machines that could spin and weave more quickly.

From the mid-eighteenth century, inventors brought about a massive change. **John Kay's** 'flying shuttle' made weaving much faster. Then **James Hargreaves**, with his 'spinning jenny', gave the spinner the power to work sixteen spindles at once. By and large, though, spinners and weavers still worked in their own homes, making woollen cloth.

Weavers in England had made cloth that was part-cotton and part linen for some time. (The yarn was not strong enough for pure cotton cloth.) But **Richard Arkwright's** 'water frame' spun strong cotton yarn. And the 'water frame' was driven by a **water-wheel**, not by hand or foot. Arkwright and a partner started a water-driven **cotton-mill** near Derby in 1771.

Samuel Crompton's 'mule' spun fine, smooth cotton yarn. Before long, British cotton cloth was the best in the world. It was also the cheapest, because the spinning was done on machines, in **mills**. The power in the mills at first was water. In the 1790s, though, came the first cotton-mills with machines that were worked by **steam**.

Now try Exercise 4.1.

Source 4a

A woman spinning by hand in her own home in the eighteenth century

Centuries

The **eighteenth** century was the hundred years from 1701 to 1800.
The **nineteenth** century was the hundred years from 1801 to 1900.
The **twentieth** century is the hundred years from 1901 to 2000.
We call the years 1701 to 1730 the **early eighteenth century**.
We call the years 1731 to 1770 the **mid-eighteenth century**.
We call the years 1771 to 1800 the **late eighteenth century**.

Exercise 4.1

Read **Section A** and the note on 'Centuries'. Then write out the sentences, replacing the dates with 'the _____ _____ century'. The first missing word should be 'early', 'mid', or 'late'. The second missing word should be 'eighteenth' or 'nineteenth'. The first one has been done for you.

a In **1750** woollen cloth was made by country people in their own homes.
Answer: In **the mid-eighteenth century** woollen cloth was made by country people in their own homes.
b James Hargreaves invented the 'spinning jenny' in **about 1765**.
c In **1779** Samuel Crompton invented the 'mule'.
d In **the 1780s** most cotton-mills used water power.
e By **1820** a lot of cotton-mills were using steam engines.
f Cotton cloth was Britain's main export in **1850**.
g The price of cotton cloth fell in **the 1880s**.

B 'King cotton'

Cotton mills spread through **Lancashire** in the first years of the nineteenth century. (A second, smaller cotton district grew up in Scotland.) At first, as many of the mills had water-wheels as steam engines. But by 1840 nearly all were driven by steam.

Soon after 1800, Britain was making as much cotton cloth as wool. By 1830, cotton was miles ahead. Cotton was popular because it was fine, light in weight, and easy to wash. Above all, it was cheap – the new machines, and low wages in the mills, meant that the prices steadily fell.

Until 1820, cotton exports went mainly to Europe and the U.S.A. After that, though, much more went to India and the Far East. By 1850, cotton cloth was Britain's biggest export, and India was her biggest market. Cotton was 'king' in Lancashire. The port of **Liverpool** thrived, importing raw cotton from the U.S.A., and exporting finished cloth.

Until the 1830s, most of the weaving was done by **handloom weavers**, working at home or in their workshops. They were well paid – in 1805 they got 23 shillings (£1.15) a week. Then, after 1830, power looms and weaving mills began to take over. Handloom weavers' wages crashed to six shillings (30p) a week.

The woollen industry also changed to machines and mills. But here the changes came later. Until 1830, most of the spinning and weaving was still done by hand. By 1850, though, spinning was done mainly in the west Yorkshire mills. Weaving took another 20 years to follow suit.

Now try Exercise 4.2.

Source 4b

Spinning with 'mules' in a Lancashire cotton mill in 1834. The boy in the bottom right of the picture is sweeping beneath the machine while it is working.

'The Dinner Hour' – factory girls outside a mill in Wigan in 1874

Exercise 4.2

Read **Section B**, and look at **Sources 4a** and **4b**.
Write out the notes, filling in the blank spaces.

Things that changed between 1750 and 1850:

a _____ was done on a wheel in 1750, and on a 'mule' in 1850.

b _____ engines were used to drive machines in cotton mills.

c The _____ of cotton cloth fell.

d _____ became Britain's main market for cotton cloth.

e The wages of _____ _____ fell to almost nothing.

Things that did not change between 1750 and 1850:

f Britain continued to make a lot of _____ cloth.

g Most _____ of woollen cloth was still done by hand.

C Factory children

Mill owners said that they had to keep their prices down. That was why workers' hours had to be long, and wages low. Women and children got lower wages than men, so the owners employed a lot of women and children. (Look at the **cartoon**.)

Children as young as six or seven worked up to fourteen hours a day in the mills. Their pay was about three shillings (15p.) a week. Many were killed or injured by the moving parts of the machines they had to clean. Others were maimed by a foreman's fist or strap. Sadly, many of them were forced to work by their own parents. Their fathers were out of work, and the family needed the few shillings that they could earn.

Some decent employers paid their workers a fair wage. Some even built good houses for them, and ran schools for their children. Some mill-owners took part in a movement for factory reform. Most mill-owners were against the reformers, though. They said that shorter hours for children would put up their costs, and bring them to ruin.

Mill-owners did not obey Parliament's first acts cutting mill hours. But an act passed in 1833 said that inspectors would enforce the law. The act banned all children under nine from cotton mills. Children over nine were allowed to work, but there were strict controls on their hours. By 1847, ten hours per day was the limit for boys and all female workers.

Now try Exercises 4.3 and 4.4.

Source 4c

Don't come to me with the old tale that the rich know nothing about the hard life of the poor. If they don't know they ought to know. We are their slaves as long as we can work. We pile up their fortunes with the sweat of our brows. Yet we live as separate as if we were in two worlds.

Words spoken by a character called John Barton in the novel *Mary Barton*, written by Elizabeth Gaskell in 1848.

Women and children working in a cotton mill

Source 4d

As you enter the factory, the whirring of a million hissing wheels hits your ears. Then you see the hundreds of helpless children. They have lost all trace of health, joy, and youth. Lean and crooked limbs, pale and sunken cheeks, dim and hollow eyes make them look old before their time. Neither these little slaves nor the whirling spindles they serve ever stop – the foremen, straps in hand, are watching all the time.

Adapted from a novel, *Michael Armstrong*, written by Mrs. Trollope in 1840.

Source 4e

There are now 145 men, 217 women, and 795 children employed at New Lanark mills. The children are well fed – they get oatmeal porridge with milk twice a day, barley broth for dinner, and either beef or cheese. They begin work at six in the morning, and stop at seven at night. Those under nine years old do not work at all. There is a school for the children – those under nine attend in the day-time, and the others after work.

Adapted from an account written by William Lockhart in 1795.

The division of workers in cotton mills in 1835

Children under 14 years old.

Young people between the ages of 14 and 18.

Men over the age of 18.

Women over the age of 18.

Exercise 4.3

Read **Section C** and **Sources 4c**, **4d**, and **4e**. Ask these questions about each of the sources. Make the answers into a chart.

a Who wrote it?
b When was it written?
c What kind of book or paper does it come from? Do you know the title?
d Is it fact or fiction?

Exercise 4.4

Discuss these questions in a group:

a What do **Sources 4b**, **4c**, **4d**, and **4e** tell us about factory conditions?
b What do the sources tell us about the opinions of workers and bosses?
c Can you think of any reasons for saying that **i** these sources give us a good idea of factory life; **ii** they may give a false impression?

Either give your answers as talks to the class, or make a group tape.

5 Canals and Roads

A collier unloading coal in the Thames near Deptford. A painting by Samuel Scott.

A Colliers and barges

As industries grew, more heavy loads of iron and coal had to be moved from place to place. As towns grew, they had to have more food and fuel. Moving heavy loads in horse-drawn wagons on bad roads was slow and expensive. It was much cheaper to send them by **water**.

Hundreds of small ships with cargoes of corn and wool sailed from port to port along the coasts. Ships called **colliers** carried coal from the Tyne to London. As London grew, so the number of colliers grew as well. Other loads went by river. Gangs of men worked on the Trent, Severn, and Thames, making them deep enough to take barges of iron and cloth.

It was a short step from rivers to **canals**. England's first canal was the **Sankey Cut**, from St. Helens to the River Mersey. It was opened in 1757, to let barges carry coal from the Lancashire mines to Liverpool.

A canal from the **Duke of Bridgewater's** coal-mine at Worsley to Manchester (seven miles away) was opened in 1761. Its engineer, **James Brindley**, became famous, and his canal was the engineering wonder of its day. Part of it ran in a tunnel into the mine, and part was on an **aqueduct** over the River Irwell. Barges on the canal carried the duke's coal cheaply to Manchester — the price of coal there was cut by half.

Now try Exercise 5.1.

Source 5a

The Barton Aqueduct in 1794

Source 5b

The canal passes over the River Irwell at Barton bridge. It is carried by a strong, thick, stone bridge, consisting of three arches. The centre arch is 63 feet wide and 38 feet above the surface of the water. The bridge is high enough to let the largest barges on the Irwell go through with their masts and sails standing.

Adapted from a book written by John Aikin in 1795.

it deep
ough yet?

Glug!

Exercise 5.1

Read **Section A** and **Source 5b**, and look at **Source 5a**.

a Make notes on the Barton aqueduct:

   i Which details can we learn from **Source 5a**, but not from **Source 5b**?

   ii Which details can we learn from **Source 5b**, but not from **Source 5a**?

   iii Which details can we learn from both sources?

b Draw a picture of the Barton aqueduct.

A canal joins the River Severn at Stourport

25

B Canal mania

After 1770, canals began to snake their way through much of England. (Look at the **map**.) Engineers like Brindley planned the routes, with all their locks and tunnels. Men with picks and shovels did the digging. They were called 'navigators' (or 'navvies') because they dug the 'navigations'. The work was hard, but the wages were good.

Canals were expensive to build. The men who **invested** money in them had to be rich. They hoped that canals would make them big profits, and some of them were right. The profits came from the tolls paid by the firms whose barges used the canals. For many investors, canals also meant cheap transport for their own goods (e.g. coal, cloth, or corn).

Owners of coal-mines, cotton-mills, and iron-works used canals because they were far cheaper than the roads. (One horse could pull a canal barge loaded with 50 tons of coal. A horse could draw only two tons of coal by road.) The great potter **Josiah Wedgwood** was both a canal-user and an investor. (Smooth canals were far better for his wares then bumpy roads.)

In the 1790s there was a mad rush to invest in new canals. It was the time of 'canal-mania'. Too many canals were built, and a lot of investors lost money. But good schemes still made profits. The Leeds to Liverpool canal, finished in 1816, was a great success. Then traffic began to decline as the railways spread in the 1830s and 1840s. In some areas, though, canal barges continued to carry coal until well after 1900.

Now try Exercises 5.2 and 5.3.

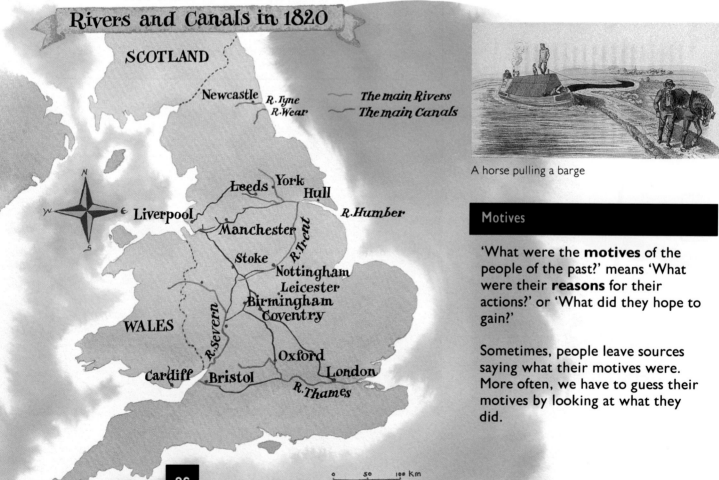

Rivers and Canals in 1820

SCOTLAND

Newcastle R.Tyne R.Wear

—— The main Rivers
— The main Canals

Leeds York Hull
Liverpool R.Humber
Manchester R.Trent
Stoke
Nottingham
Leicester
Birmingham
Coventry
WALES R.Severn
Oxford
Cardiff Bristol London
R.Thames

0 50 100 Km

A horse pulling a barge

Motives

'What were the **motives** of the people of the past?' means 'What were their **reasons** for their actions?' or 'What did they hope to gain?'

Sometimes, people leave sources saying what their motives were. More often, we have to guess their motives by looking at what they did.

Exercise 5.2

Read **Section B** and the note on 'Motives'. Think of suitable ways to complete the sentences. Write out the whole sentences.

a The motive of the 'navvies' was probably _____ .

b All investors in canals wanted to make _____ .

c Many investors also got cheap _____ .

d Owners of coal mines used canals because _____ .

e Josiah Wedgwood's motives were _____ .

Exercise 5.3

Write out the sentences. Fill in the blank spaces (two in each sentence) with words from this list:

    early   mid-   late   eighteenth   nineteenth
    twentieth

a James Brindley built the Bridgewater canal in the _____ _____ century.

b A lot of canals were built in the _____ _____ century.

c There was a period of 'canal mania' in the _____ _____ century.

d The Leeds to Liverpool canal was completed in the _____ _____ century.

e Canals began to decline in the _____ _____ century.

f Some canals were still used in the _____ _____ century.

C Turnpikes and stage coaches

Canals were built partly because the roads were so bad. Most roads were just tracks, with huge ruts and potholes. When it rained, coach wheels sank in the mud. Before 1700, no-one built new roads. It was the job of each parish to mend its roads, but not much work was ever done.

In the eighteenth century, Parliament passed laws to set up **turnpike trusts**. Each trust had the right to take charge of a stretch of road. It could charge tolls at toll-gates, and was supposed to repair and improve the road. Some trusts bought land, and built completely new roads.

By 1830, about 20,000 miles of Britain's roads belonged to turnpike trusts. (More than 120,000 miles were still in the hands of the parishes.) Not all the trusts did good work — some just collected tolls and left the roads as bad as before. But some trusts employed engineers to plan and build new roads and bridges.

Two famous road-builders were **Thomas Telford** and **John Macadam**. Telford used the same methods as the Romans — firm foundations and packed layers of stone and gravel. Macadam's roads were simpler — he relied on the weight of the traffic to press stones and chips into a solid surface.

Through the work of Telford, Macadam, and others, some roads were much improved. Regular **stage-coach** services became possible. (The coaches changed horses at coaching-inns after each eight or ten-mile 'stage'.) By 1832, the coach from London to Edinburgh took only two days. In 1754, the same journey took ten days.

Now try Exercises 5.4 and 5.5.

Source 5c

From Preston to Wigan (in Lancashire) there is a turnpike, but I do not know words that can describe this road. I warn travellers to avoid it like the devil. They are almost bound to break their necks or their limbs on it. They will find ruts four feet deep, full of mud after a wet summer. The only mending it gets is when they throw in some rough stones.

Written by Arthur Young in 1770.

Source 5d

The turnpike from Salisbury to Romsey (in Wiltshire and Hampshire) is the best I ever saw. The trustees of that road look after it really well. The surface is smooth, and there are no loose stones, ruts or pools of water. It is wide enough for three coaches to pass each other, it is straight, and it has an even grass verge the whole way.

Written by Arthur Young in 1768.

Source 5e

The turnpike from Tyburn through Uxbridge (in Middlesex) has more heavy wagons on it than any road in England. Yet all last winter there was only one decent track on it. That was less than six feet wide, and eight inches deep in mud. The rest of the road was at least a foot deep in mud. It was crowded with broad-wheeled wagons, drawn by as many as ten horses.

Written by John Middleton in 1798.

A stage-coach

Exercise 5.4

Read **Section C** and **Sources 5c**, **5d**, and **5e**. Write out the sentences, and write TRUE or FALSE after each of them.

a All turnpike trusts built new roads.
b All turnpike trusts charged tolls, but some did not improve the roads.
c The only bad turnpikes were in the north of England.
d Arthur Young must have travelled round England.
e Arthur Young liked the Salisbury to Romsey road.
f All the roads leading out of London were good.
g The Tyburn to Uxbridge road was so bad that no-one used it.

Exercise 5.5

Write sentences to show that you know what these words and terms mean:

colliers   aqueduct   navvies   investors
canal-mania   potholes   turnpike trust   toll-gate
road engineers   stage-coaches

6 Railways and Ships

Euston station in London in 1837

The opening of the Canterbury and Whitstable railway, 1830

A The first railways

Before the year 1700, trucks ran on wooden rails in the Cornish tin mines. On Tyneside, truck-loads of coal ran on wooden or stone tracks. By the late eighteenth century, in some places, the rails were iron. All the trucks on these 'waggonways', of course, were drawn by horses.

By 1800, fixed steam engines were working at many coal-mines, pumping and winding. The next step was to make a **locomotive** – a moving steam engine that would pull trucks of coal. Many men worked on the idea. The most successful was a Tyneside mine engineer, **George Stephenson**. An engine which he built in 1814 pulled coal trucks to and from the docks.

The first **railway** which carried passengers as well as coal was opened in 1825. It linked **Stockton** and **Darlington** and its engineer was Stephenson. He used locomotives, but not for the whole route. For part of the way, fixed engines pulled the trucks with cables.

More important was the **Liverpool** to **Manchester** railway. George Stephenson was its engineer. At an engine trial in 1829, he had proved that steam locomotives worked, and that his were the best. And when the railway opened in 1830, the people were thrilled by its speed and comfort. In its first year, 400,000 passengers used it.

Now try Exercise 6.1.

Source 6a

The Liverpool to Manchester railway was opened on Wednesday last. They say that the trains will be able to travel at sixteen to eighteen miles an hour. That would cut by half the time the journey takes. The people here talk of having breakfast at home, travelling each way by train, and getting home for dinner. Before long we shall have railroads all over England.

Adapted from *The Observer* newspaper, 19 September 1830.

Source 6b

What will happen to men who have put money into turnpikes? What will become of the coach-makers, coachmen, and inn-keepers? What about the men who breed horses and the harness-makers? Do you realise how much smoke and noise these railway engines will make, rushing past at ten or twelve miles an hour? They will frighten the cattle grazing in the fields. They will destroy the peace and quiet of gentlemen's estates.

Part of a speech made in the House of Commons in the 1830s.

Source 6c

Building the Britannia Bridge over the Menai Straits (between North Wales and Anglesey) in 1849

Exercise 6.1

Read **Section A** and **Sources 6a** and **6b**, then answer the questions.

a Was the author of **Source 6a** in favour of railways or against them?

b According to **Source 6a**, what was the best thing about railways?

c Was the author of **Source 6a** right about the future of railways?

d Was the author of **Source 6b** in favour of railways or against them?

e The author of **Source 6b** said that which people would lose their jobs?

f According to **Source 6b**, what was the worst thing about railways?

g Who do you think wrote **Source 6b** – a landowner, a mill-owner, or a merchant?

B The railway age

After 1830, there was a rush to build railways. London and Birmingham were linked in 1838. By 1850, all the main cities were connected. 'Navvies' did the work, laying track, building bridges, digging tunnels. In twenty years or so, the face of Britain was changed.

In the 1840s, investors rushed to buy shares in railways. (It was just like the 'canal mania' of the 1790s.) Once again, not all the plans were wise, and some fortunes were lost. And there were crooks – **George Hudson**, the 'railway king', swindled lords and bankers out of vast sums.

Most of the railways used the '**standard gauge**' – the lines were 4 feet 8½ inches (1.43 metres) apart. But the Great Western Railway's engineer, **Isambard Kingdom Brunel**, used the '**wide gauge**' of seven feet (2.13 metres). He said it gave passengers a smoother and safer ride. A law passed in 1847 made all new lines use the standard gauge. But the Great Western did not change until 1892.

The railways took a lot of trade from the canals, and killed the stage-coaches. Busy coaching-inns became quiet country pubs. Strangely, though, the spread of railways led to more demand for horses. The horses pulled the coaches and carts that took people and goods to the stations.

Railways had a huge effect on jobs. As well as the 'navvies' who built them, there were the drivers, guards, porters, etc. who ran them. Then there were the engineers who made the locomotives and coaches. (New towns, such as Swindon and Crewe, grew up around the railway works.) Thousands of men worked making the iron for the track, bridges, and rolling-stock. And thousands of miners were employed digging the coal that the railways used.

Now try Exercises 6.2 and 6.3.

Source **6d**

I began work on the railways when I was nine. My first job was greasing wagons, then I drove horses. After that, I was a navvy on the London to York line. I got 2s.9d. (14p) a day there, but only four days' work a week. Then the work stopped, and I was sacked. I got jobs on other lines, but last March I was paid off again. I sold all my tools to buy food, and now I don't know what to do. I'm only twenty-seven, but I'm dead beat.

The words of a navvy, reported by Henry Mayhew in 1861.

Source **6e**

Men came from all over to work as navvies. They were experts in digging ditches, sinking wells, and boring tunnels. Each gang of men agreed the price for a job with the boss before they started. They could work twelve or sixteen hours at a stretch, with only short stops for meals. Danger meant nothing – the bigger the risk the keener they were to do the job.

Adapted from a book written in 1861 by Samuel Smiles, who would have seen navvies at work.

Source 6f

Navvies at work on the Liverpool to Manchester railway

Primary and secondary sources

Letters and books written by people who were present when events happened are called **primary sources**. Words spoken by people who took part in events are also primary sources. So are drawings made at the time.

Papers and books written by people who were **not** present are called **secondary sources**. The authors of secondary sources must have heard about the events from someone else, or read about them in books.

Exercise 6.2

Read **Section B** and **Sources 6d** and **6e**, and look at **Sources 6c** and **6f**. Read the note on 'primary and secondary sources'.
Write two sentences about each of the sources:

a Say what the source tells us or shows us.
b Say whether it is a primary or a secondary source.

Exercise 6.3

Write a short essay about **Sources 6d** and **6e**.

a What do they tell us about navvies and the kind of life they led?
b What differences are there between what the two sources say?
c Why do you think that **Sources 6d** and **6e** give different pictures of the navvies' lives? (Try to think of more than one reason.)

Right: A souvenir postcard of a steamer at Helensburgh in Scotland in the 1880s

Below: The famous clipper, the 'Cutty Sark'

C Sailing ships and steamships

The first boats with engines were **paddle-steamers**. The engine drove two paddles, one on each side of the boat. In the early days, they worked only on rivers and lakes. But in the 1820s steamers were running between England and France. Experts agreed, though, that steamers could not make long voyages — there would be no room for all the coal they would need.

A steam paddle-boat did cross the Atlantic in 1819. But this was not a real victory for steam, as the boat used sails for most of the way. **Brunel** (see **Section B**) began a steamer service from Bristol to New York in 1838, but his ships also used sails as well as steam.

Sailing ships took a long time to die. In the mid-nineteenth century, the **clippers** were fast and cheap to run. Each year, they raced to bring the new

Brunel's 'Great Eastern' in 1858

season's crop of tea from China to England. After 1869, when steamers took over the China trade, clippers still carried wool from Australia. Even in 1900, a fifth of British ships still used sails.

From the 1850s, Britain began building ships of iron, and later steel. Iron ships could be bigger – Brunel's 'Great Eastern', built in 1858, was 19,000 tons, five times as large as the biggest wooden ships. Iron ships with steam engines began to take charge of the world's trade. Most of them were built in British yards. By 1900, Britain had a big lead as the world's first shipping and shipbuilding nation.

Now try Exercise 6.4.

Exercise 6.4

Find out the dates of the events below. (They are all in this chapter.) Write the dates and events in the right places on a time chart. The chart should be divided into two sections, 'Railways' and 'Ships'.

Stephenson made the first successful locomotive.
Opening of Stockton to Darlington railway.
Opening of Liverpool to Manchester railway.
Opening of London to Birmingham railway.
Law saying that new lines had to use the standard gauge.
Great Western Railway changed to standard gauge.
First paddle steamer crossed the Atlantic.
Brunel began steamer service from Bristol to New York.
Brunel's 'Great Eastern' launched.
Steamers took over the China trade.

Draw a picture of either an early locomotive or an early steam-boat.

7 Britain and the French Revolution

Marie Antoinette, the queen of France, on her way to the guillotine in 1793

A   Guillotines in London?

In the eighteenth century, the king of **France** was the real ruler of his country. There was no parliament to help make the laws. Many Frenchmen thought that this was wrong. In the **Revolution** which broke out in 1789 they demanded a share of power and fair rights for the people.

Men and women in Britain were shocked by the violence of the French Revolution. But some of them (called the 'radicals') were on the side of the French reformers. They thought that Britain also needed a good deal more freedom. They said that rule by king, lords, and gentry was unfair. They wanted all men to have the right to vote.

By 1792 most towns in Britain had radical clubs. But the news in 1793 turned the British people against the French. The king and queen of France were put to death in public on the **guillotine** in Paris. Hundreds of nobles and ordinary men and women came to the same end. Horror swept through Britain. Radicals, it was said, were the friends of murderers.

The outbreak of war with France in 1793 made things worse for the radicals. Now their enemies called them traitors as well. The government banned radical meetings, closed down their clubs, and arrested their leaders. They said that those who took the radicals' side wanted guillotines in the streets of London.

Now try Exercises 7.1 and 7.2.

Source 7a

The execution of King Louis XVI of France, January 1793

Exercise 7.1

Read **Section A**, then copy and complete the sentences.

a The French reformers wanted _____ .

b People in Britain who took the side of the French reformers were called _____ .

c British radicals wanted _____ .

d British people turned against the French when they heard that _____ .

e Radicals were accused of being traitors when _____ .

f The British government attacked the radicals by _____ .

Source 7b

Last night in a London coffee-house, a foreigner jumped up and started to make a speech. He called the king (of England) a tyrant, and the people slaves. He said that in nine months' time the Jacobins of Paris would bring freedom to London. At this, an English gentleman seized him, gave him a horse-whipping, and kicked him out of the house.

Adapted from *The Observer* newspaper, 27 May 1792. [Mass executions took place in France when the 'Jacobin' party took power.]

Source 7c

Yesterday morning King Louis XVI was put to death in the Square of the Revolution in Paris. The scaffold was high for all to see, and the houses round the square were full of women, looking out of the windows. The king took leave of his priest, but was not allowed to make a speech. His head was cut off straight away, and the blood-thirsty Jacobins waved their hats in the air, shouting 'God save the nation!'

Adapted from *The Observer* newspaper, 27 January 1793.

Exercise 7.2

Read **Sources 7b** and **7c**, and look at **Source 7a**. Write out the sentences, and write either TRUE or FALSE after each.

a There were foreigners in London in 1792.
b The French hoped that a revolution would break out in Britain.
c Well-off English gentlemen were on the side of the French Revolution.
d Executions took place in public in Paris.
e Soldiers were on guard round the guillotine.
f French people did not show much interest in the execution of the king.
g Those about to die were allowed to make speeches.
h Jacobins were against all kings.

B The threat of invasion

In 1793, France was at war with most of the countries of western Europe. Her enemies planned to march into France, take Paris, and bring the Revolution to an end. But the French fought hard and drove the invaders out. Then they went on the attack themselves. Britain sent an army to Holland to help the Dutch, but it too was beaten.

One by one, the nations of Europe made peace with the French. Britain did not have to give in, for she had the sea and her navy to protect her. At sea, the Royal Navy won a string of victories. The bold and clever Admiral **Nelson** became a national hero.

Britain's trade made her rich enough to afford the world's strongest navy. She was also able to give money to other states to pay for their armies. But on land the French always beat them. One reason was that they had the best generals. The ablest of them was **Napoleon Bonaparte**. In 1804, he made himself **Emperor** of France.

Bonaparte crossing the Alps

35

Britain and the French Revolution

In 1805 Napoleon gathered a huge army and a fleet of boats on the north coast of France. He tried to trick the Royal Navy into leaving the Channel clear. But the plan failed. And a few months later Nelson crushed the fleets of France and Spain (France's ally) in the Battle of **Trafalgar**. Nelson was killed in the battle, but Britain was safe from invasion.

Now try Exercises 7.3 and 7.4.

Source 7e

A British cartoon from 1805 – John Bull (standing for Britain) challenges 'Boney' (Napoleon Bonaparte) to try to invade

Taking Sides

People often take sides – they are for one party, or they support one team. Men and women in the past took sides as well. The author of **Source 1c** (page 5) was for enclosures, but the women in **Source 1b** were against them. **Sources 6a** and **6b** (page 30) give two different views of railways. Artists could take sides also, as you will see if you look at **Sources 7d** and **7e**.

A French cartoon from 1804 – invasion of Britain by sea, by air, and through a tunnel

Source 7f

'John Bull goes to war' – a set of cartoons drawn in 1793

36

Exercise 7.3

Read **Section B** and the note on 'Taking Sides'. Study **Sources 7d** and **7e**. Write two paragraphs, answering these questions:

a How can you tell that **Source 7d** was drawn by a French artist?

b How can you tell that **Source 7e** was drawn by a British artist?

Exercise 7.4

Study **Source 7f**, then answer the questions in sentences.

a Who do you think 'John Bull' is meant to be?

b When did these events occur?

c What happened to John Bull?

d What happened to John Bull's family?

e What do you think were the artist's opinions? (Write more than one sentence if you can.)

C Napoleon and Wellington

Between 1805 and 1807, Napoleon's armies again crushed the great powers – Austria, Prussia, and Russia. He took land from them to add to his French empire. (Look at the **map** on page 38.) He made one of his own brothers King of Holland, and another King of Spain.

Napoleon tried to beat Britain by cutting her trade. He passed a law which said that the parts of Europe controlled by France must not trade with Britain. Since most of Europe was under French rule, this would have cut Britain's merchants off from their markets. But smugglers got round the law, so it did not do Britain much harm.

The French invaded **Portugal** to make her obey the trade law. But the British sent an army to help the Portuguese. In 1812, the British troops, led by the **Duke of Wellington**, advanced from Portugal to **Spain**. In the next year, they and the Spanish drove the French out of Spain as well.

Also in 1812, Napoleon fell out with the Tsar (emperor) of **Russia**. He sent a huge army (500,000 men) to teach the Tsar a lesson. The Russian army did not beat the French, but the Russian winter did. Hundreds of thousands of Frenchmen died in the cold on the long retreat from Moscow.

Now all of Europe rose against Napoleon. He was beaten, and had to give up his throne. The allies sent him to the island of **Elba**. But he escaped and returned to France. In a last battle at **Waterloo**, in 1815, the Duke of Wellington, with Prussian help, beat the French. Napoleon spent the rest of his life as a prisoner on the island of **St. Helena** in the South Atlantic.

Now try Exercise 7.5.

Napoleon's Empire in 1812

Moscow•

North Sea

UNITED KINGDOM

London•

RUSSIA

PRUSSIA

GRAND DUCHY OF WARSAW

CONFEDERATION OF THE RHINE

Ruled by Napoleon

Allies controlled by Napoleon

0   200   400   600   800   1000 Km

Paris•

Vienna•

AUSTRIA

Atlantic Ocean

FRANCE

ITALY

Rome•

TURKISH EMPIRE

PORTUGAL

Madrid•

SPAIN

NAPLES

Mediterranean Sea

THE CAUSES OF NAPOLEON'S DEFEAT

Britain had command of the - - - - . Nelson won Battle of - - - - - - - - .

Napoleon quarrelled with the - - - - of Russia.

The Spanish rebelled when Napoleon made his - - - - - King of Spain.

French tried to cut off Britain's - - - - - with rest of Europe.

Napoleon lost nearly 500,000 men when he invaded - - - - - - .

War in - - - - and Spain (British led by Duke of - - - - -).

Napoleon forced to surrender in 1814. Escaped and beaten at - - - - - - in 1815.

Exercise 7.5

Read **Section C**. Then copy out the chart on the causes of Napoleon's defeat, with or without the cartoons. Fill in the blank spaces in the boxes.

8 The Reform of Parliament

The polling booth –
an election in the
eighteenth century

A Rule by property-owners

In the eighteenth century, Britain was ruled by its great landowners. Most of them were nobles — members of the **House of Lords**. The leaders of the gentry (smaller landowners) sat in the **House of Commons**. They were less important than the lords, and often followed their lead.

The members of the House of Commons (M.P.s) were elected, but not by all the people. On the whole, only better-off men had the right to vote. (All the men could vote in a few towns.) No women could vote. And voting was in public. So landlords often **told** their tenants who to vote for. Men who could not be forced to vote the right way would be bribed.

Each **county** and **borough** in England had two M.P.s. Boroughs were supposed to be the most important towns. But some of them were '**rotten boroughs**' — villages with only a few voters. These voters obeyed their landlords. So it was the landlords who chose the M.P.s. On the other hand, some large towns, such as Birmingham, did not have their own M.P.s.

The **radicals** (see Chapter 7) wanted to get rid of rotten boroughs, and to give all men the vote. But the lords and gentry said that only men who owned property should be able to vote. And the lords and gentry were in control. During the wars with France (1793 to 1815) they said that the radicals were no better than the French Jacobins.

Now try Exercise 8.1.

B The 1832 Reform Act

The radicals were just a small group. The main parties were the **Tories** and the **Whigs**. The Tories were a party of lords and gentry, and strongly against the reform of Parliament. The Whigs were a mixture of landlords and businessmen. They thought that **some** reform would be wise. But until 1830 the Tories were in power, so Parliament stayed unchanged.

At last, in 1830, the Whigs formed a government. In 1831, they brought in a bill to abolish some rotten boroughs and give more men the vote. The Tories voted against it. But the people wanted reform — there were riots in London and Bristol in favour of the bill. In the end, it was passed and became the **1832 Reform Act** (i.e. a new law).

The Reform Act abolished 56 rotten boroughs and gave towns such as Birmingham, Manchester, and Leeds the right to have their own M.P.s. It

---

Exercise 8.1

Read **Section A**, then copy and answer the questions.

a Which group of men ruled Britain in the eighteenth century? _____

b Who had the right to vote in the eighteenth century? _____

c Why was there so much bribery in elections? _____

d How many M.P.s did each English county have? _____

e Boroughs were supposed to be what? _____

f Which two things did radicals want? _____ and _____

g The lords and gentry thought that which people ought to have the right to vote? _____

Aye, I thought this Rotten Rubbish would make a fine Dust!

gave middle-class men in towns and the richer tenant-farmers the right to vote. But there were no votes for the working class.

The Reform Act gave the vote to about half a million men. Now, one man in every five could vote. But there was no secret ballot. So men could still be forced or bribed to vote as their landlords wished. The landowners still had more power than anyone else.

Now try Exercises 8.2 and 8.3.

Lord Grey (The Whig Prime Minister) sweeping away the rotten boroughs

Source 8a

The middle class have grown richer and stronger. Now they want the House of Commons to be reformed, so that they can have a share of the power that the nobles have at present. If we are wise, we will give in to their just demands before it is too late. If we do not, there will be riots and revolution, as there were in France.

From a speech made in the House of Commons by Thomas Macaulay in 1831.

Source 8b

The present House of Commons could not be improved. Its members are all men of property, and most of them own land. I think that is as it should be. So I am against any kind of reform. And so long as I am a member of the government, I will oppose reforms which other men propose.

Adapted from a speech made by the Duke of Wellington in the House of Lords in 1830. The Duke of Wellington was Prime Minister at the time.

Exercise 8.2

Read **Section B**, and read again the note on 'Motives' on page 26. Read **Sources 8a** and **8b**.

a Which of the speakers (Thomas Macaulay and the Duke of Wellington) do you think voted in favour of the Reform Bill, and which voted against it? (Write two sentences.)

b What do you think were Thomas Macaulay's motives for saying what he did? (Choose two sentences from the list below.)

c What do you think were the Duke of Wellington's motives for saying what he did? (Choose two sentences from the list below.)

   i He thought that the House of Commons was perfect.
   ii He wanted to avoid riots and revolution in England.
   iii He wanted to give votes to the working class as soon as possible.
   iv He thought that most M.P.s should be landowners.
   v He wanted to give the rich middle class a share of power.

Source 8c

An election in Tonbridge in Kent, December 1832

Source 8d

Fizkin's side have got 33 voters in the lock-up coach-house at the White Hart Inn. They keep them locked up there till they want them (to vote). That stops us getting at them. And even if we could, it would be no use, for they keep them very drunk. Smart fellow, Fizkin's agent.

Adapted from *Pickwick Papers*, a novel written by Charles Dickens in 1837.

Fact and fiction

Fiction sources (novels and stories) do not describe events that actually happened. But that does not mean that they are useless to the student of history. Descriptions of events and places in novels often tell us a great deal about how things were in the past.

Exercise 8.3

Read the note on 'Fact and fiction' and **Source 8d**, and look at **Source 8c**.

a Write notes on **Sources 8a, 8b, 8c** and **8d**. Say who spoke, wrote, or drew them, and when. Which sources are fact, and which is fiction?

b What do **Sources 8c** and **8d** tell us about elections in the 1830s? (Write a paragraph.)

c Is the fiction source useful to the historian? Can you find anything in **Sections A** and **B** to make you think that you should believe the fiction source? (Write a paragraph.)

C **Rule by the people**

Not everyone was happy with the Reform Act. The **Chartists** (see Chapter 13) wanted votes for all men. Later, the trade unions took up the same call. By 1866, the leaders of the main parties agreed. The **Conservatives** (who had been called Tories) passed a second Reform Act in 1867. The **Liberals** (formerly Whigs) passed a third one in 1884.

The 1867 Act gave the vote to working-class men in the towns. Farm labourers had to wait until 1884. But after the third Reform Act, most men could vote. (Women could not vote until 1918.) Also, from 1872 voting was secret. This meant that voters no longer had to follow the orders of their landlords or employers.

The Reform Acts took Britain well on the way to **democracy** – rule by the people. Some of the lords and gentry

were alarmed and afraid. They thought that working men were too ignorant to have the vote. They expected wild men with crazy ideas to be elected as M.P.s. They said that rich men's property would be taken away.

In fact, the working men voted for Conservatives or Liberals, and there was no revolution. (There were very few working-class M.P.s at first, though.) The biggest change was that after 1832 the House of Commons was more important than the House of Lords. The party that won most seats in the Commons formed the government. So after the Reform Acts, the **people** chose their government.

Now try Exercises 8.4 and 8.5.

Source 8e

We, the working classes of Britain, are denied our basic rights. We pay most of the taxes, but we are not allowed a share in choosing those who fix the taxes. We obey the laws, but we do not elect the men who make the laws. So let us join together to demand votes for all men, and the secret ballot. Let us respect the law and march forward to our freedom.

From a speech by Edmund Beales, president of the Reform League, in 1865.

Signing a petition in favour of votes for working men

Exercise 8.4

Read **Section C** and **Source 8e**. Answer the questions in sentences.

a Which two 'basic rights' did the speaker in **Source 8e** demand?
b The speaker said that people who pay taxes deserve what?
c He said that people who obey the law are entitled to what?
d Did he urge his audience to riot and break the law?
e Is **Source 8e** a primary or a secondary source? Give a reason for your opinion. (If you are not sure, look again at the note on page 32.)

Exercise 8.5

Write sentences to show that you know what these words and terms mean:

nobles   gentry   bribe   rotten borough
Tories   Whigs   act   secret ballot   democracy

9 The Move to the Towns

A The growth of population

The first **census** (official count of people) in Britain took place in 1801. After that, there was a census every ten years. For the years before 1801, experts have made **estimates**. They have studied the records of births and deaths that are kept in churches. Put together, their results and the census figures give the graph which you see on page 45.

The graph shows that the population of England and Wales began to rise in the mid-eighteenth century. By 1901, it was six times as large as in 1750. What the graph does not show is that the rise was much faster in some places than others. In Lancashire, west Yorkshire, and the west Midlands, the population grew very fast indeed. In other words, it grew fastest in regions where there was a lot of **industry**.

Historians agree that the population grew. But they do not agree on **why** it grew. Some say that the main cause was that more babies were born. Some think that the main cause was that people lived longer. Most experts think that it was a mixture of the two. What is clear is that the rise in population took place at the same time as the growth of industry.

Now try Exercises 9.1 and 9.2.

Between 1815 and 1860, seven million people *emigrated* from the British Isles. Most of them went to the USA, Canada, and Australia. Cartoons like this told them that they would have a better life abroad.

HERE AND THERE:
OR, EMIGRATION A REMEDY.

Exercise 9.1

Read **Section A** and study the **graph**. Then draw a timeline from 1750 to 1900. Divide the timeline into centuries and parts of centuries (early, mid, late). Mark the following on the time-line:

  i Population of England and Wales began to grow.
 ii The first census.
iii Population of England and Wales reached 10 million.
 iv Population of England and Wales reached 15 million.
  v Population of England and Wales reached 20 million.
 vi Population of England and Wales reached 30 million.

Source 9a

After 1740 people lived longer, so the population grew. This was because:
  i *Farmers could keep more cattle, because they had turnips to feed them on in winter. The result was more meat for people to eat.*
  ii *People were more healthy because they ate bread made from wheat, not from a mixture of wheat, barley, and rye.*
  iii *People washed more, partly because soap became cheaper.*
  iv *Cotton became cheap, and cotton clothes are easy to wash.*
  v *New houses were warmer and healthier. They were built of brick or stone, not wood and clay. Their roofs were tiled, not thatched.*
  vi *Doctors became more skilled, and there were more hospitals.*

Ideas adapted from a book written by Professor T. S. Ashton in 1947.

Source 9b

After 1740 the population grew.
  i *There was not so much disease about, because:*
  a *Houses were more healthy. They were built of brick instead of wood and clay, and had tiled roofs instead of thatch.*
  b *Brown rats drove the black rats out of the towns and cities. Plague germs were carried by black rats' fleas.*
  c *It may be true that people washed more.*
  ii *Fewer people died of hunger – harvests were good, so bread was cheap.*
  iii *In the towns, there were more jobs and higher wages. So young men and women got married earlier and had more children than before.*
  iv *Doctors learned more, but very few people could afford doctors. Hospitals were more likely to spread disease than cure it.*

Ideas adapted from a book written by Miss P. M. Deane in 1965.

Growth of population in England and Wales

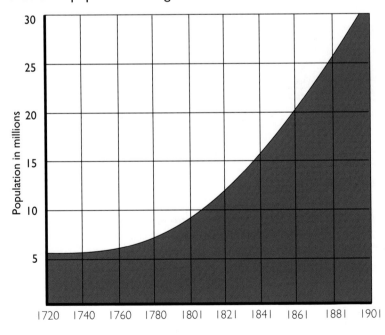

Exercise 9.2

Read **Sources 9a** and **9b**. Each source gives a list of reasons why the population grew, but the two lists are not the same. Write notes to show:

a Which ideas appear in both lists. (The words are not exactly the same.)
b Which ideas appear in **Source 9a**, but not in **Source 9b**.
c Which ideas appear in **Source 9b**, but not in **Source 9a**.
d Which point the two sources disagree about.

B Towns and cities

With the spread of industry, Britain's towns and cities got bigger. London and the great ports continued to grow. Mill towns like Oldham and Rochdale appeared from nothing. In 1800, two-thirds of the population still lived in the countryside. By 1850, the figure was down to a half. By the 1890s, three-quarters of Britain's people lived in towns.

The first reason for this change was that men and women moved from the country into the towns. They came to work in the factories and mills. The wages were low, but better than labourers could get on the farms. The second reason was that families were large. It was a good thing to have a lot of children if five and six-year-olds could earn money in the mills.

Workers' houses were thrown up quickly and cheaply. A lot of them were two or three-roomed 'back-to-backs'. They stood in rows in narrow streets or clustered round gloomy courtyards. Many families lived in a single room. Most streets were not paved, and the only sewer was an open drain. Water was piped from the river to a pump in the street or yard.

Bad housing and impure water led to disease, of course. People died much younger in the towns than in the countryside. **Cholera** was common — an outbreak in London in 1849 killed 13,000 people. **Typhoid fever** threatened not only the poor in the slums — it killed Prince Albert, Queen Victoria's husband, in 1861.

Now try Exercise 9.3.

Source 9c

The street was unpaved. A gutter ran down the middle, with pools every now and then. Women from their doors tossed household slops into the gutter. The slops ran into the pools, and lay there, stagnating. Passers-by had to step on the heaps of ashes to keep their feet clean.

Adapted from the novel *Mary Barton*, written by Elizabeth Gaskell in 1848.

Source 9d

Dudley Street in the Seven Dials district of London in 1872

Source 9e

Houses were built back-to-back along narrow alleys, or round the four sides of a court or yard. The only entry to the court was a tunnel. Towns grew too fast for these houses to be connected with the water-supply. So the people had to buy from the water-carriers, who sold water by the pail.

Adapted from a book written by Professor J. D. Chambers in 1961.

Spectators looking at the gas lights in Pall Mall in 1809

Can we believe the sources?

You need to be careful when you are using history sources. You should ask questions about the people who wrote or made them. For example: Did the author who wrote the source (or the artist who drew it) know how things really were? Did he write about (or draw things) that he had seen himself? Did he read lots of sources and look at all kinds of evidence? Did he have any reason for not telling the truth?

Exercise 9.3

Read **Section B** and **Sources 9c** and **9e**. Look at **Sources 9d** and **9f**. Read the note 'Can we believe the sources?' Then discuss these questions in a group:

a What do the sources tell us about town streets in the nineteenth century? (And why is **Source 9f** so different from **Source 9d**?)
b What reasons are there for **i** believing, and **ii** not believing what each of the sources tells us?
Either give short talks telling the rest of the class what you think, **or** make a group tape.

C Health in the towns

Before 1830, the government did not think that the state of the towns was its business. Local councils could improve things or not, as they wished. In fact, some did so. Birmingham and Manchester had some paved streets by 1800. Glasgow and London had gas street-lights by 1815.

The first big change was an act to reform the **councils** in 1835. It said that they had to be elected by the men who paid the rates. And it gave them the power to provide water supplies and systems of sewers if they wished. In some places, big improvements followed. In others they did not — ratepayers did not like councillors who spent a lot of money.

By the 1840s, people knew that there was a connection between bad sanitation and disease. And the government in London was growing

Charles Pierce, one of the first Metropolitan policemen, in 1850

MICROCOSM dedicated to the London Water Companies BROUGHT FORTH ALL MONSTROUS, ALL PRODIGIOUS THINGS, HYDRAS AND GORGONS, AND CHIMERAS DIRE, Vide Milton

MONSTER SOUP commonly called THAMES WATER, being a correct representation of that precious stuff doled out to us !!!

A cartoonist's view of London water in the mid-nineteenth century. People in London and elsewhere were forced to drink untreated water which led to the spread of disease.

A new block of flats built to replace some of London's slums

more and more alarmed about people's health in towns. From 1848, it passed a string of acts urging the councils to take action. In the end, it said that they had to pave and light their streets, provide sewers, and see that new houses had proper water supplies.

The nation's health slowly improved. But there was not much change in housing. An act passed in 1875 said that councils could buy slums, pull them down, and build new houses for the people. Birmingham council made good use of the act, but not many others followed its lead. In 1900 far too many working people still lived in slums.

Now try Exercise 9.4.

Exercise 9.4

Read **Section C**. Copy the sentences and write TRUE or FALSE after each one.

a Before 1830, the government took no interest in improving towns.

---

b No town councils made any improvements before 1830.

---

c The way local councils were elected was reformed in 1835.

---

d After 1835 all councils laid on supplies of pure water.

---

e In 1840 doctors knew that open sewers were a danger to health.

---

f After 1848 the government tried to improve the people's health.

---

g In 1875 the government forced councils to pull down slums.

---

h All town councils built better houses for the people.

10 Making Ends Meet

Source 10a

'The Harvest Home'. At the end of the harvest, the farmer leads his workers home to a celebration feast.

A The standard of living – the evidence

The '**standard of living**' of a family depended on how much money came in and how high the prices were. If father got a pay rise, they could afford better food, clothes, and shoes. In other words, the standard of living rose. If father lost his job, the standard of living fell.

We do not know enough about the standard of living in the past. We know how high the wages were in some trades, but not all. We know about the rise and fall in the price of bread. But we do not know enough about the price of clothes, or rent. We know that wages were high in some parts of Britain, and low in others. We know that the unemployed suffered, but not who was unemployed, or for how long.

The **weather** had a lot to do with the standard of living. If it was good, there was a good harvest, and the price of **bread** was low. A bad harvest meant a shortage, and a high price. Bread was working people's main food — they sometimes had cheese with it, but seldom got meat.

The things that working people bought are clues to their standard of living. By the year 1850, their bread was made from pure wheat, not the cheaper mixture of wheat, barley, and rye that they had eaten before. Also, tea and sugar sales had greatly increased. (In the early eighteenth century, only the rich could afford tea and sugar.) By 1875, working people were spending far more on bacon, jam, chocolate, and beer.

Even at a time when the standard of living was rising, there were years of bad harvest and high unemployment. Food riots in 1795, 1812, and 1830 tell us a lot about the farm labourers' standard of living in those years. High unemployment in the late 1830s was the chief reason why so many working people backed the Chartists. (See Chapter 13.)

Now try Exercises 10.1 and 10.2.

Deductions from evidence

The **evidence** (what we know about the past) does not always tell us everything we would like to know. But we can often **make deductions** from the evidence (work things out from the clues we have). For example:
Corn prices were very high in the 1790s. **Therefore**, there must have been a shortage of corn.
Therefore, the harvests must have been bad. **Therefore**, the weather must have been bad.

Exercise 10.1

Read **Section A**, then copy out the following sentences and use these words to fill in the blanks:

fell   higher   price   rent   rose
unemployed   wages

a If wages _____ the standard of living improved.
b If prices rose, the standard of living _____ .
c We do not know how high the _____ were in all trades.
d We have some information about the _____ of bread.
e Wages were _____ in some areas than others.
f We do not know how much _____ people paid for their homes.
g We do not know how many people were _____ .

Exercise 10.2

Read the note 'Deductions from evidence', and use paragraphs 3, 4, and 5 of **Section A**. Look at **Sources 10a** and **10b**. Then copy and complete the sentences.

a Harvests were important for the standard of living, because _____ .
b The fact that people changed to pure wheat bread tells us that _____ .
c If working families could afford tea and sugar, _____ .
d People do not spend money on jam and chocolate if _____ .
e The food riots in 1830 tell us that _____ .
f In **Source 10a**, we can tell that it had been a good harvest, because _____ .
g The villagers in **Source 10b** must have done so much knitting because _____ .

Source   **10b**

The Wensleydale knitters (1814). Men, women and children in Wensleydale in Yorkshire spent every spare moment knitting stockings. They needed the extra money because farm workers' wages were so low.

B The rising standard of living, 1750-1875

Working people's standard of living rose between 1750 and 1793. Harvests were mainly good, so bread prices were fairly low. Labourers had money to spare for new clothes, as well as food. And from the 1780s, the new cotton mills were making cheap cloth.

During the long wars with France (1793 to 1815) it became harder to make ends meet. Britain imported less wheat from abroad, and prices rose. Also, there were bad harvests in the mid-1790s and in 1811-12. On the other hand, wages were quite high at this time, and unemployment was rare.

From 1815 to 1850, wages fell, but prices fell even more, so people were better off. Some were not so lucky, though. The wages of **handloom-weavers** (see Chapter 4) fell far more than prices. And there were spells of unemployment that hit most trades. Since no work meant no pay at all, unemployment brought great hardship.

From 1850 to 1875, prices were rising, but wages were rising faster. New factories, mills, mines, and ship-yards were taking on people. Thousands of workers left the land, where wages were low, and took better-paid jobs in the growing towns. Standards of living were higher than ever before.

Now try Exercise 10.3.

Not everyone was prosperous in this period. On the left is a family of match-box makers in London in 1871. Below is a poor family of cotton workers in Manchester in 1862.

Exercise 10.3

Read **Section B**. The notes below refer to four different periods of time. Write the notes in the right order, and add the dates.

a Prices and wages both fell, and there were spells of unemployment.

b Prices and wages both rose, and most working people were quite well off.

c Wages were high, but so were prices, and the standard of living did not rise.

d Harvests were good, prices were low, and the standard of living was rising.

C The Poor Law

Before 1900 there were no old-age pensions or free health service in Britain. And there were no state payments for those too sick to work or for the unemployed. Instead, there was the **Poor Law**. This was meant just for the very poor — the old, the sick, and the starving.

Each **parish** had an 'overseer of the poor'. His job was to collect **rates** from the heads of households (most men in the parish). He used the money to help those in need. (But he had to be careful not to give out too much!) If they wished, parishes could join together, build **workhouses**, and make the old, the sick, and orphans live in them.

The parish of **Speenhamland** in Berkshire began 'topping-up' the wages of low-paid farm workers in 1795. This 'system' soon spread through most of southern England. It had two very bad effects — the farmers paid even lower wages than before,

and the poor rates had to go up to meet the cost.

The act which Parliament passed in 1834 was meant to make the Poor Law cheaper. It said that groups of parishes had to build workhouses. In future, 'able-bodied' poor would get help only if they came into the workhouses. And workhouses were made unpleasant, to discourage idlers. The food was poor, discipline was strict, and families were split up.

Poor rates were cut by half after the 1834 act, and rate-payers were pleased. But poor people hated the workhouses. And the new law did not really work. In times of slump and high unemployment, there was no room in the workhouses for all those who needed help. So they were given 'out-relief' — they got Poor Law money while they stayed at home.

Now try Exercise 10.4.

Husbands and wives were separated in the workhouse

Source 10c

The mill-owner got the children, at the ages of six, seven, and eight, from the workhouses of Edinburgh. It was his duty to feed, clothe, and educate them, and he spared no expense in doing this. Their rooms were clean and airy, and there was plenty of food. But to meet the costs of all this, he had to make the children work in the mill from six in the morning to seven at night. Their schooling began when they had finished work.

Written by Robert Owen about New Lanark mill in about 1800. [When they were old enough, workhouse orphans were apprenticed to tradesmen.]

Source 10d

When she was ten years old, her mother died. As there was no-one among her friends that was rich enough to save her from the workhouse, to the workhouse she went. Three months later, she and many others were sent as apprentices to Deep Valley factory. They were supposed to go there to learn a good trade, but in truth they went as slaves.

Adapted from the novel *Michael Armstrong*, written by Mrs. Trollope in 1840.

Source 10e

A notice was pasted on the outside of the gate next morning. It offered a reward of five pounds to anybody who would take Oliver Twist off the hands of the parish. In other words, five pounds and Oliver Twist were offered to any man or woman who wanted an apprentice . . .
. . . Mr. Gamfield, the chimney-sweep, smiled as he read the notice. Five pounds was just the sum he wanted. As to the boy, Mr. Gamfield knew that a workhouse boy would not need much to eat.

Adapted from the novel *Oliver Twist*, written by Charles Dickens in 1839.

Exercise 10.4

Read **Section C** and **Sources 10c**, **10d**, and **10e**.
Write short paragraphs, answering the questions below.

a What were supposed to be the duties of employers who took on workhouse orphans as apprentices?
b Why were some employers quite keen to take on workhouse orphans?
c What do you think about the education mentioned in **Source 10c**?
d Which of the sources are fact, and which are fiction? Should we believe what the fiction sources say? If so, why?

11 Free Trade

A Tariffs and Corn Laws

All governments need to collect **taxes**. Some are on the wages people earn (income-tax), and some on what they buy. For most of the eighteenth century, the government's money came mainly from **tariffs** (customs duties). These were taxes on imports, such as tea, silk, and brandy. But **Adam Smith** said that tariffs reduced trade, and so harmed Britain. He was in favour of **free trade**.

In the 1780s, the government did reduce some tariffs. But during the wars with France, from 1793 to 1815, it needed more money, so tariffs went up again. Then in the 1820s they were cut once more, but Britain was still a long way from free trade in 1830.

There were always tariffs on corn imports in the eighteenth century. But the **Corn Laws** passed in 1815 **banned** imports if the price of corn in Britain was less than £4 per quarter. The **motive** was to keep the farmers' pro-

Workers and mill-owners versus farmers and landowners

fits up, so that they could pay high rents to the landowners.

Merchants and mill-owners did not like the Corn Laws. In 1838 a group of them formed the **Anti-Corn Law League**. They said that the Corn Laws put up the price of bread, and that if they were **repealed** (abolished), the price of bread would fall. Workers' wages could then be reduced, so British-made goods would be cheaper, and there would be more trade.

The government did not give in straight away. But in 1842, **Sir Robert Peel**, who was then Prime Minister, made a big cut in tariffs. (He brought in an income-tax at the same time.) Then in 1846 came famine in Ireland. (See Chapter 14.) The Irish needed cheap food, so Peel **repealed the Corn Laws**. The move split Peel's party, the Conservatives, but it made Britain a free trade nation.

Now try Exercises 11.1 and 11.2.

Source 11a

The aim of the Anti-Corn Law League is to abolish the Corn Law. This law is a tax on corn, a tax to help the land-owners. If we can get rid of it, all the other taxes on trade will follow. We will then have Free Trade, which will make all nations better off. Not only that, but it will also lead to peace and goodwill, and an end to war and conquest.

Adapted from a speech made by Richard Cobden in 1840. Cobden was one of the leaders of the Anti-Corn Law League.

Source 11b

When news reached Ashton-under-Lyne that the Corn Laws were repealed, flags were raised in all parts of the town. The flags had slogans on them, such as 'Free trade for ever', and 'Free trade with all the world'. Outside a barber's shop was a flag saying 'No supporters of the Corn Laws shaved here'. Some of the mill-owners have held feasts for their workers.

Adapted from a report in *The Times* newspaper, 3 July 1846.

Exercise 11.1

Read **Section A** and **Sources 11a** and **11b**, then copy and answer the questions.

a 'Tariffs' is another name for what? _____ _____

b Adam Smith was in favour of what? _____ _____

c What happened to tariffs in the 1820s? _____

d **Source 11a** says that the Corn Laws were meant to help whom? _____

e **Source 11a** says that free trade will end what? _____

f Which new tax did Sir Robert Peel start in 1842? _____

g When were the Corn Laws repealed? _____

h Who were the main employers in Ashton-under-Lyne (**Source 11b**)? _____

i Why do you think the people of Ashton-under-Lyne were so pleased about the repeal of the Corn Laws? _____

Exercise 11.2

Answer these questions about **Sources 11a**, **11b**, **11c**, and **11d**:

a Who wrote it (or said it)?
b When was it written or said?
c Is it a primary or a secondary source?

Write your answers out in a chart.

John Bright and Richard Cobden (left and centre) were the leaders of the Anti-Corn Law League

B The 'workshop of the world'

By 1860 there were hardly any tariffs left, and free trade was almost complete. Even though bread prices did not fall, the years after 1850 were a time of success for Britain. In 1873 her exports were worth £240 million a year, nearly five times what they were in 1842.

Britain, with her mills and factories, produced far more goods, and much more cheaply, than any other nation. Britain invented railways, and was the first country to have a railway system. By the 1850s, she was exporting railway lines and engines to the rest of the world. She was right to call herself the 'workshop of the world'.

But Britain's **imports** grew also. Her population had grown so fast that she needed to import a lot of her food. Most of her raw cotton came from the U.S.A. A growing share of the wool and iron ore she used was coming from abroad. By 1870, Britain was paying more for her imports than she was earning from her exports.

A large part of the difference was made up by the money earned by the **merchant navy**. After 1850, trade was growing all over the world. More than half of it was carried in British ships. By 1890, Britain's merchant navy was as big as all other merchant fleets combined.

Now try Exercise 11.3.

Miners in 1871 cutting coal by hand. They are using Davy lamps. You can also see a pit-pony and a boy employed to look after it down the mine.

Source 11c

The typical Englishman was still a farm-hand in 1831. And most of those who worked in industry in 1831 were employed in small workshops, not factories. By 1851, more people lived in towns. . . . But still only a quarter of the workers were employed in factories and mines.

Adapted from a book written by Professor J. D. Chambers in 1960.

Do they agree or disagree?

Authors sometimes **appear** to disagree with each other, when in fact they do not. If we read what they say carefully, we can see that they may **both** be right. The authors of **Sources 11c** and **11d** **appear** to disagree about Britain in the mid-nineteenth century. But is that really the case?

Source 11d

By 1830 Britain was mining 75 per cent of Europe's coal, and making more than half of its cotton goods. By 1860 she was producing 54 per cent of the world's iron and steel. The volume of her trade was going up all the time. . . . She truly deserved to be called 'the workshop of the world.'

Adapted from a book written by Martin Roberts in 1972.

Exercise 11.3

Read **Section B**. Read the note 'Do they agree or disagree?' and read **Sources 11c** and **11d very carefully**.
Then discuss these questions in a group:

a Does **Source 11c** say that Britain was **not** producing a lot of coal, cotton, and iron?
b Does **Source 11d** say that **most** British workers were employed in mines, mills, and factories?
c Does **Source 11c** make you think that the number employed in factories and mines was growing?
d What does **Source 11d** tell us about industry in other countries?
e Do the two sources disagree with each other?
f What do the two sources together tell us?

Either give talks, telling the rest of the class what you think, or make a group tape.

C The Great Exhibition

It was **Prince Albert's** idea to hold a festival of arts and science in London, and he played an important part in the planning. On 1 May 1851, the **Great Exhibition** was opened by Queen Victoria. It took place in the **Crystal Palace**, a huge structure of iron girders and glass plates, built for this one event in Kensington Gardens. The 'palace' was 550 metres long, and more than 40 metres high.

The first aim of Prince Albert and the planners was to display the arts and

The outside of the Crystal Palace

Queen Victoria opening The Great Exhibition in the Crystal Palace on 1 May 1851

industry of all nations. Out of this came their second aim, to show that Britain's industry was the best. This, they hoped, would prove the value of free trade. And free trade, as Richard Cobden said, brought world peace. (See **Source 11a**). Lastly, it would be a great show to entertain and inform the public.

Entries came from all over the world. Visitors liked the chinaware from France and the lace from Spain. But it was British industry that impressed them most. Never had there been such a show of human skill. British workers, it was said, were the 'working bees of the world's hive'.

The exhibition was open for five months. In that time, 6,000,000 visitors saw it. Thousands came up to London on special trains. A trip to the Crystal Palace was everyone's idea of a day out in 1851. Queen Victoria was so thrilled that she came back 30 times.

Now try Exercise 11.4.

Some of the exhibits in The Great Exhibition

Exercise 11.4

Read **Section C**.

a Plan an essay on 'The motives of the men who planned the Great Exhibition of 1851'. Write brief notes saying what each paragraph would be about — one paragraph for each motive.
b Draw a picture of the outside of the Crystal Palace.

12 The End of British Prosperity?

A The decline of agriculture

A quarter of all British men were farm workers in 1850. Britain's **agriculture** was still her most important trade. But industry was growing all the time. And after 1875, farming hit bad times.

Food from abroad was the main cause of the decline of agriculture. As her population grew, Britain had to import more of her food. And by the 1880s, imported **wheat** (mainly from the U.S.A.) was cheaper than wheat grown in England. British farmers could not get a decent price for the crops they grew.

Why was wheat from the U.S.A. cheaper to buy in London than wheat grown 20 miles away in Essex? The first answer is that land was very cheap on the American prairies. (English

A grain import store on the Thames in 1880

farmers had to pay rent.) Secondly, there were more machines (e.g. binders and steam ploughs) in the U.S.A., so they did not need so many men. And thirdly, with railways and steamships, transport costs were low.

Low prices meant low profits for farmers. Landlords had to charge lower rents, so they were worse off too. Many farmers stopped growing wheat, and kept cattle and sheep instead. Then, in the 1880s and 1890s, frozen mutton and beef began to arrive from abroad, and meat prices fell as well. A lot of farmers went out of business. Those who did not needed fewer labourers. Farm workers and their families made for the towns.

Now try Exercise 12.1.

Source 12a

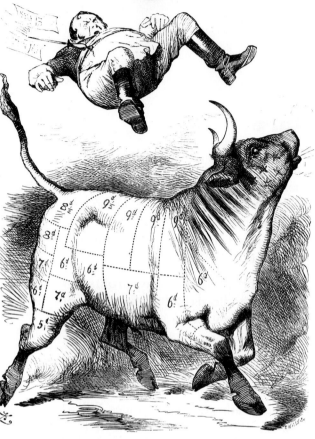

'John Bull and American beef' – John Bull (the English butcher) is trying to sell English beef at 15d (15 old pence, or 6 new pence) a pound. The most expensive cut of American beef is only 9½d (4 new pence) a pound.

Source 12b

Unloading a cargo of American meat at Liverpool in 1877

Exercise 12.1

Read **Section A**, and study **Sources 12a** and **12b**.
Write TRUE or FALSE after each of the sentences.

a Coal-mining was Britain's most important trade in 1850.
b The decline of British farming took place after 1875.
c Cheap wheat from America made prices fall in Britain.
d American farmers did not have to pay high rents for land.
e British landlords did not suffer from the decline in farming.
f **Source 12b** shows a cargo of frozen meat from America.
g **Source 12a** shows the British butcher suffering from American competition.
h In **Source 12a**, John Bull is being 'thrown' because his meat prices are too high.

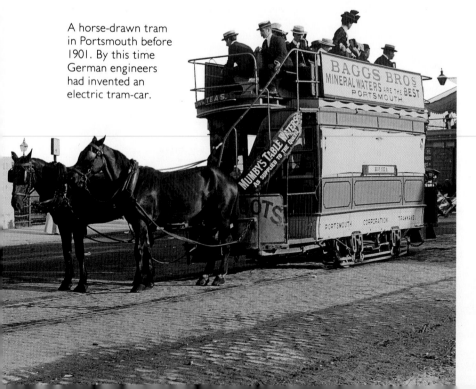

A horse-drawn tram in Portsmouth before 1901. By this time German engineers had invented an electric tram-car.

B Good news and bad

Low food prices were good news for most workers. For those with jobs, the standard of living rose between 1870 and 1900. But not everyone had a job. And spells of unemployment brought hunger and misery.

It was the age of coal. Steam engines drove machines in factories and mills. Every home had a coal fire. Railways, with steam engines, were the main form of transport. Towns and cities were blackened with smoke. All this was good for miners and mine-owners

– coal output almost doubled between 1870 and 1900.

A lot of coal was sold abroad, but the chief export was still cotton cloth. Britain, though, was no longer the only country with cotton mills. Now there were **competitors** in Europe and the U.S.A. And most of these foreign makers of cotton were using new machines. The British mills kept to their old machines, which were starting to become out-of-date.

A worse sign was that Britain no longer led the world with new inventions and ideas. The **Germans** were the leaders in the **chemical** industry (making dyes for textiles, for example). And it was a German who invented the **petrol engine** and the first **car**. Until 1896 cars were allowed on British roads only if a man with a red flag walked in front.

In the late nineteenth century, inventors found ways of making **steel** in large amounts. Steel took over from iron in machines, bridge girders, and ships. Some of the steel-making inventions were British. But more steel was made in Germany and the U.S.A. than in Britain.

Now try Exercise 12.2.

An early car in the 1890s

Exercise 12.2

Read **Section B**, then copy the sentences and fill in the blanks.

a For workers who had _____ the standard of living rose after 1870.

b Industry's main fuel in the nineteenth century was

_____

c The numbers of jobs for _____ nearly doubled between 1870 and 1900.

d _____ _____ remained Britain's main export.

e Mills in _____ and the _____ were now making cotton cloth.

f A _____ invented the petrol engine and made the first car.

g Both Germany and the U.S.A. were making more _____ than Britain.

Now draw a picture of a car of the 1890s.

C Why did Britain lose her lead?

Britain had been the world's leader in industry and trade. Why did she let Germany and the U.S.A. catch up? Part of the answer is that she could not stop them. The U.S.A. is far bigger and richer than Britain. In the end, it was almost bound to take the lead.

At the same time, some British firms were badly **managed**. By the 1880s and 1890s, a lot of them were run by the sons and grandsons of the men

who set them up. And the sons and grandsons, too often, never went near the mills and factories. They just lived off the profits.

To keep up with their rivals, firms need to **invest** money. (For example, they have to buy more up-to-date machines.) The money comes from the firm's own profits or from well-off **investors**. But after 1870, British investors put more money into foreign railways and mines than they put into British factories and mills. They got good **dividends**, but they did not help British industry. In fact, they helped foreign firms to grow.

British firms which sold machines abroad also helped Britain's rivals. Foreign mills, full of British-made machines, made good, cheap cloth. Then they sold it to customers who, 30 years before, had bought from Britain.

On top of this, Britain stuck to free trade, while most other countries did not. The French and Germans put **tariffs** on imports to **protect** their own industries. French tariffs on imported cloth made British-made cloth expensive in France. So French people bought French-made cloth instead.

Lastly, British inventors were falling behind. Had this something to do with education? German schools and universities led the world in science and engineering. But young men in Britain's 'public schools' studied Latin and Greek and not much else. Most of them knew no science at all.

Now try Exercises 12.3 and 12.4.

Source 12c

A British cartoon in 1885 against free trade. The combination of British free trade and foreign tariffs on British imports is helping our competitors and crushing British industry and workers.

Exercise 12.3

Read **Section C.**

Divide a page into two halves, left and right. In the left-hand half, write down the five causes below.

a Some British owners did not visit their mills and factories.

b Not enough money was invested in British factories and mills.

c British firms supplied machines for foreign cotton mills.

d Many countries put tariffs on exports from Britain.

e Pupils in British schools did not learn much science.

In the right-hand half, write down a **result** opposite each cause.

Source 12d

A depression began in about 1875. By 'depression' we mean that profits fell and unemployment rose. There were three main causes:

1 Our factories and mills produced more than they could sell.

2 Foreign countries brought in tariffs and ended free trade.

3 Foreign competition made it harder to sell our goods, at home and abroad.

Adapted from the report of a Royal Commission on trade, 1886.

Source 12e

India is the most important market for our cotton cloth. So long as we keep control of the seas, the 250 million people there will be ready to take our produce. At present we sell them cottons to the value of two shillings (10p.) per head per year. This could easily be increased to six shillings. If we did that, it would be very good for the British working man.

Adapted from a speech made by Sir Richard Temple, M.P. in 1887.

Source 12f

You will find that your clothes, and your wife's, are made from cloth that was woven in Germany. Your children's toys and dolls were made there too. Your newspaper is printed on paper that came from Germany. Go where you like in your house and you will see the same "Made in Germany" mark. It is on the piano in your drawing room and the mug on your kitchen dresser. It is even on your drain-pipes and the poker for your fire.

Adapted from a book written by E. E. Williams in 1896.

Exercise 12.4

Read **Sources 12d, 12e,** and **12f,** and look at **Source 12c.**

a Source 12c – i Describe what you can see in the cartoon. **ii** What were the artist's **opinions** about free trade and tariffs?

b Source 12d – i What did the authors mean by 'depression'? **ii** In their **opinion**, what were the causes of the depression?

c Source 12e – i Note down any **facts** in this source. **ii** What were the author's **opinions**?

d Source 12f – i Note down at least six 'Made in Germany' items. **ii** What do you think the author's **opinions** were?

13 Working Class Movements

A From Luddites to Chartists

The British working class did not care about revolutions. Sometimes they took part in protests, but only when they were hungry or unemployed. The things that concerned them were jobs, wages, and the price of bread.

The '**Luddites**' who smashed knitting and spinning machines in 1811 did not want to cut the king's head off. They were afraid of losing their jobs — they said that the machines put them out of work. The crowds who listened to **Henry Hunt** between 1816 and 1819 cheered when he said that all men should have votes. But what they really cared about were unemployment and high taxes. When trade improved after 1820, the troubles ceased.

The leaders of the **Chartists** were angry that the 1832 Reform Act did not go far enough. Their 'People's Charter', which they drew up in 1838, asked for votes for all men (but not women), a secret ballot, and elections every year. Between 1838 and 1848,

A Chartist demonstration at Kennington Common in London in April 1848

the Chartists got massive support from the working people. Thousands took part in their meetings and strikes. Millions signed their petitions to Parliament.

But it was jobs, wages, and prices that were the main worries of the working class. There were trade slumps in the 1830s and 1840s, and workers knew that if you lost your job there was nowhere to go but the dreaded workhouse. This was what made them follow the Chartists.

Britain's rulers did not give in to Luddites, radicals, and Chartists. They said that machine-breakers would be hanged. They cut down the freedom of the press. They banned meetings, and sent troops to break them up. These tactics worked – mill-hands could not take on the army. The last Chartist protest, in 1848, was a dismal flop.

Now try Exercises 13.1 and 13.2.

Exercise 13.1

Read **Section A**. What do you think were the **motives** of the following? (What did they want, or say they wanted?) Write your answers as notes.

a The Luddites.
b Henry Hunt.
c The people who attended Henry Hunt's meetings.
d The Chartist leaders.
e The people who followed the Chartists.

Source 13b

A crowd of 60,000 men and women gathered in St. Peter's Field, Manchester. When Henry Hunt (the radical) arrived, he brought them to silence, and began to speak. Just then, a platoon of cavalry was seen making for the platform. To get through the mass of people, they drew their swords and struck out to right and left. A company of hussars came to their aid. The crowd panicked and fled, chased by the soldiers with drawn swords. Eleven persons were killed, and several hundred injured.

Exercise 13.2

Read **Source 13b** and study **Source 13a**.
Copy out the sentences and fill in the blanks. (Use words from the list below.)

dressed   eleven   large   panicked   **Source 13a**
Source 13b   swords   trampled

a _____ shows us that a man tried to make a speech, but does not tell us anything about him.

b Only _____ says that the speaker was a radical.

c Only **Source 13b** tells us how _____ the crowd was.

d Only **Source 13a** shows us how the soldiers were _____.

e Both sources tell us that the soldiers drew their _____.

f Both sources tell us that the crowd _____.

g Only **Source 13a** shows us that some people were _____ by the horses.

h Only **Source 13b** tells us that _____ people were killed.

Five of the 'Tolpuddle Martyrs', who were allowed to return to England from Australia in 1838

B Early trade unions

The first trade unions were set up between 1700 and 1750. Most of them were like the guilds of the Middle Ages. Members paid in a few pence a week, and got help if they were unemployed or ill. Strikes were rare, but they were not unknown. The miners of Tyneside went on strike in 1765.

Employers did not like the unions. Some used **lock-outs** to try to smash them. (They closed their works, and gave the men their jobs back only if they left the union.) And the government took the employers' side. In 1799, during the wars with France, all unions were banned by law.

In spite of the ban, some unions kept going, often in secret. When the ban was lifted, in 1824, new unions were set up. Most of them soon failed, though — employers locked the men out, and brought in non-union workers. And wages were low, so not many men could afford union fees.

Robert Owen tried to set up a union for all trades and for the whole of England in 1834. But it lasted only a few months. It collapsed when six farm workers from Tolpuddle in Dorset were charged with taking a secret oath when they joined it. They were found guilty and sentenced to seven years' transportation to Australia.

News of the '**Tolpuddle Martyrs**' killed Owen's union. Workers did not want to risk transportation for themselves and ruin for their families. For the 'martyrs', though, the outcome was not all bad. Fair-minded people wrote letters and signed protests, saying that they had been wrongly treated. After four years, the 'martyrs' were brought home.

Now try Exercise 13.3.

A meeting of 50–60,000 Trade Unionists at Copenhagen Fields in 1834, to carry a petition to the king, asking for the release of the Tolpuddle Martyrs

Exercise 13.3

Read **Section B**. Then draw a timeline from 1700 to 1850. Mark these events in the correct places on the timeline, with dates if you know them.

a Robert Owen's union was set up.
b War with France began. (See Chapter 7.)
c War with France ended. (See Chapter 7.)
d Tyneside miners went on strike.
e The 'Tolpuddle Martyrs' were allowed to return home.
f The first trade unions were set up.
g The last Chartist protest took place. (See Section A of this chapter.)
h Trade unions were banned by law.
i The end of the ban on trade unions.

A lock-out against the union

C 'New unions'

The unions of the 1840s were small, and most of them did not last long. But in the 1850s the first of the 'new unions' were set up. Like the early unions, they were for **skilled** workers, such as engineers, iron founders, and joiners. They were 'new' in that they were **national** — their members came from all parts of Britain.

The new unions helped their members when they were ill or unemployed. They looked after former members' widows and orphans. They tried to **persuade** employers to pay higher wages. They tried to get the government to give more rights to unions and their members. They had some success — the 1867 Reform Act gave the vote to working men in towns. And an act in 1875 said that

strikes were legal, so long as **pickets** were peaceful.

By the 1870s, most skilled trades had unions. The next step was unions for **unskilled** workers. And there were strikes for better wages. The London match girls won their strike in 1888, and so did the London dockers in 1889. But a miners' lock-out in south Wales in 1898 ended in defeat.

In 1874, for the first time, two working men took their seats in the House of Commons — as **Liberal** M.P.s. The first independent **Labour** member was elected in 1892. But it was only in 1900 that the trade unions decided to set up their own party. Even then, it did not become the **Labour Party** until 1906.

Now try Exercise 13.4.

The girls who worked in Bryant and May's match factory in London went on strike in 1888. The public supported them and they won their case.

Source **13c**

Until the 1890s, trade unions were content to follow the Liberals. But in the 1890s this changed when the Liberals would not pick working men to stand for Parliament. At the same time, some employers were banding together to fight the unions. And the law courts took the employers' side. Also, more and more workers wanted someone to speak for them. All of these things were causes of the birth of the Labour Party.

Ideas taken from a book written by Professor W. Ashworth in 1960. [Not Professor Ashworth's words.]

The banner of the Amalgamated Society of Engineers, 1852

Source **13d**

In the last ten years of the nineteenth century trade was bad. At the same time, employers, with the help of the law courts, were trying to reduce the rights of the unions. For these reasons, workers began to say that there should be a party to take the side of the working class.

Adapted from a book written by Martin Roberts in 1972.

Exercise 13.4

Read **Section C** and **Sources 13c** and **13d**. Answer the questions in sentences.

a The first working men in Parliament belonged to which party?
b Which source tells us why the union leaders became unhappy with the Liberals?
c Why did the unions fall out with the Liberals?
d Which source tells us that trade was bad? When was trade bad?
e What do both sources say about the courts?
f What else were employers doing to fight the unions?
g What did workers begin to say in the 1890s?
h Which source mentions the birth of the Labour Party?

14 Ireland

Protestant landlords owned most of the land in Ireland. They lived very comfortably on the rents paid by their Irish tenants.

Inside the house of a quite prosperous Irish tenant farmer

A The Act of Union

In 1750, three-quarters of the people in Ireland were **Catholics**. But the **Protestants** (who were partly English) had all the power. They owned most of the land. Only they could hold the top jobs in the state. Only they could vote, or be members of the Irish Parliament, which met in Dublin. In any case, the Irish Parliament was forced to take orders from the government in London.

Irish Catholics got the right to vote in 1793. But they still complained that they were treated unfairly. In 1796, when Britain and France were at war, the Irish rose in revolt. (**Wolfe Tone**, their leader, was a Protestant.) The French tried to help, but storms at sea broke up their fleet. By 1798, British troops had crushed the rebels.

In 1800, Parliament passed an **Act of Union**. The act closed the Irish Parliament. Instead, Ireland was to have 100 M.P.s in the House of Commons in London. **William Pitt**, the Prime Minister, wanted to give Catholics equal rights to Protestants. But the king, George III, would not agree. So Ireland lost its Parliament, and did not get much in return.

In the 1820s, a great public speaker called **Daniel O'Connell** was the Irish leader. He said that there should be equal rights for Catholics. He meant that they should be free to be M.P.s, mayors of towns, judges, etc. The people were soon all behind him. It was clear that, if Britain did not give way, there would be civil war in Ireland. So in 1829 a **Catholic Relief Act** was passed, giving O'Connell most of what he asked for.

Now try Exercise 14.1.

Exercise 14.1

Read **Section A**, then answer the questions.

a What was the religion of most people in Ireland?
b Could Catholics be members of the Irish Parliament?
c Who led the Irish revolt in 1796?
d Who tried to help the Irish rebels?
e Which act closed down the Irish Parliament?
f Which king refused to let Catholics have equal rights?
g Who led the Irish protests in the 1820s?
h When did Parliament pass an act allowing Catholics to be M.P.s?

B The Great Famine

Ireland was a farming country. It had fertile parts, where landlords and tenants grew corn and raised cattle. But in the barren west, the peasants lived in rough cabins on tiny plots of land. The men worked on the landlords' land — the wages they earned paid the rent. On their own plots, they grew **potatoes**, which were their main food, and often their **only** food.

In the autumn of 1845, disaster struck. When the peasants dug up the potatoes, they found a black, stinking mess. **Potato blight**, a fungus disease, had destroyed the tubers below the ground. Half the crop was lost in 1845. The whole crop was destroyed in 1846, and 1848 was just as bad.

Over a million peasants died of hunger or the fever which went with it. In large parts of the west and south-west of Ireland, starving people lived off raw turnips, berries, and nettles.

Starving Irish children at the time of the Great Famine

They had no money to pay the rent for their homes and land. Some landlords let them off, but some **evicted** those who could not pay.

The government set men to work on the roads to earn money for food. It opened soup kitchens. It cancelled the Corn Laws (see Chapter 11) and brought in cheap foreign corn and maize. But the problem was too big — there were not enough jobs or places in the workhouses. The government said that there was not enough money to pay for all the schemes.

Families left their homes and took to the roads in despair. Over a million hungry, evicted people **emigrated** (left their homes for good). Some made their way to England. But many braved the 'coffin ships' that crossed the Atlantic, and started new lives in the U.S.A.

Now try Exercises 14.2 and 14.3.

Source 14a

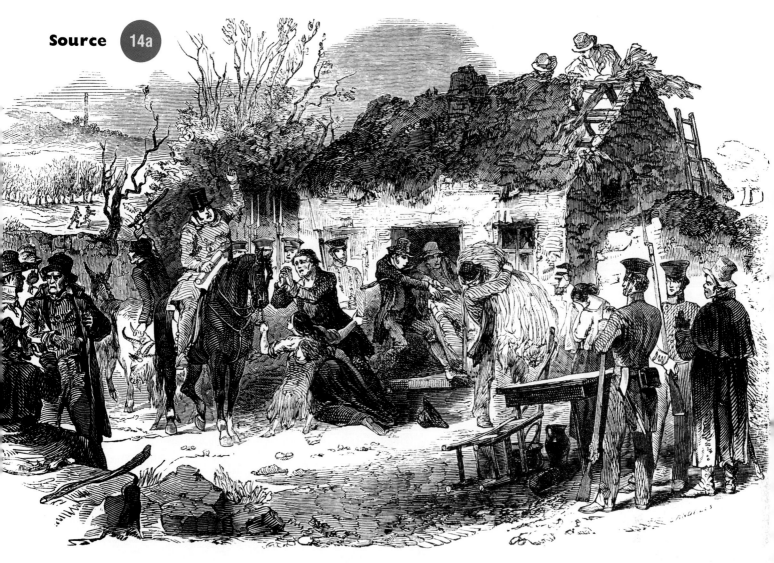

An eviction. Soldiers stand by as peasants are thrown out and their cabin is pulled down.

Source 14b

I am not easily moved, but I have to say that I was sickened by what I saw today. Crowds of women and children were scattered over the turnip fields like a flock of crows. They were eating the raw turnips, shivering in the snow and sleet. The children were screaming with hunger.

Adapted from a letter written by Captain Wynne, an English officer on duty in the west of Ireland in 1846.

Source 14c

In one place I was surprised to find the village street empty. I entered one of the cabins to find the cause, and saw six starving skeletons huddled in a corner on some filthy straw. Their only covering was a ragged cloth. As I approached, I heard a low moaning sound. They were alive, but all of them were ill with fever — four children, a woman, and a man.

Adapted from a letter written by an Irish magistrate in December 1846.

Source 14d

After the potatoes failed in 1846, the government gave eight million pounds. We hoped that the money would see the Irish through the crisis, and that they would find some other kind of food. But they just planted potatoes again. And now the potatoes have failed again. How can you help people like that? We cannot give them any more money – the result would be just the same.

From a letter written by Lord John Russell, the Prime Minister, in 1848.

Source 14e

The sheriff arrived with a strong force of police and some men with crowbars. The sheriff gave a signal, and the work began. The men dragged the miserable peasants out of their cabin. They tore the thatched roof down, and battered in the earth walls. I was only twelve at the time, but I will never forget the sight. I can still see the screaming women and the half-naked children.

An account of the events of 1848 written by Sir William Butler.

Exercise 14.2

Read **Section B** and **Sources 14b, 14c,** and **14d**.
Answer the questions in sentences. (Use your own words.)

a What sickened Captain Wynne (**Source 14b**)?
b Why were the women and children in **Source 14b** so hungry?
c Why was the village street empty in **Source 14c**?
d What were the feelings of the magistrate in **Source 14c**?
e What did Lord John Russell (**Source 14d**) think about the Irish?
f Can you think of any reasons why Lord John Russell's feelings were so different from the feelings of Captain Wynne and the magistrate? (Write more than one sentence if you can.)

Source 14f

After the eviction. A peasant family takes refuge in a ditch.

Exercise 14.3

Read **Source 14e**, and look at **Sources 14a** and **14f**.
Then write three paragraphs:

a Do **Sources 14a** and **14e** tell the same story about an eviction? Are there any differences?
b Describe **Source 14f**. What do you think has happened?
c What do you think were the opinions of the author of **Source 14e** and the artist who drew **Sources 14a** and **14f**?

C Parnell and Gladstone

The English were not to blame for the potato blight. But the Irish blamed them for not helping more during the famine. And English landlords who evicted poor peasants were hated. In the 1870s, evictions were the main cause of trouble between England and Ireland.

The Irish 'Land League' tried to protect the peasants. It organized protests and attacks on the stock and property of landlords who evicted. At the same time, Charles Stewart Parnell formed a Home Rule party. He wanted Ireland to have its own Parliament again. In the 1880s, Parnell's party won most of Ireland's seats in the House of Commons.

In England, the great Liberal Prime Minister William Gladstone tried to solve Ireland's problems. He got Parliament to pass acts which made it hard for landlords to evict peasants. He made sure that rents were not too high. But Parnell and his party were not satisfied. In the end, Gladstone decided that Ireland must have Home Rule. But not all of the Liberals agreed, and he failed to get a Home Rule bill passed.

By 1900, Parnell and Gladstone were dead. Most Irishmen still wanted Home Rule, and most of the English were against it. But there was now the question of Ulster as well. A large part of the population of north-east Ireland was Protestant. They said they were British, not Irish, and did not want Home Rule.

Now try Exercise 14.4.

Parliament rejects Gladstone's Home Rule Bill

Exercise 14.4

Read **Section C**. Find words and names in **Section C** to fit the following:

a A fungus disease which attacks potatoes.
b Peasants being put out of their homes by their landlords.
c An organization that tried to protect Irish peasants.
d A party that wanted Ireland to govern itself.
e The leader of the party that wanted Ireland to govern itself.
f A great Liberal Prime Minister of the late nineteenth century.
g A part of Ireland where a large part of the population was Protestant.

15 The British Empire in the Nineteenth Century

India in 1857

AFGHANISTAN

Kashmir

Punjab

TIBET

R. Indus

Delhi

Agra

Jaipur

Jodhpur

R. Ganges Bengal

Calcutta

Indian Ocean

Bombay

Hyderabad

Goa (Portuguese)

Mysore

Madras

Ruled by Indian Princes, protected by East India Company

Ruled by East India Company

CEYLON

0 200 400 600 800 km

British troops and Indian sepoys loyal to the British retake Delhi during the Indian Mutiny

A India

The **East India Company** (see Chapter 2) was a company with an empire. It had its own army, with British officers and Indian 'sepoy' soldiers. And by 1850, it controlled most of India. (Look at the **Map**.) Even the parts that still had rajahs and nawabs were 'protected' by Britain.

The British thought that they had brought law and order and progress to India. So they were appalled in May 1857 when the sepoy soldiers revolted and took Delhi and other towns in the north. But the British fought back, and within a year they were in control again. Both sides were guilty of many savage crimes. (See **Sources 15a** and **15b**.)

The British called it a 'mutiny'. They said that the main cause was that the sepoys did not like the new greased cartridges which they had to use. (This was to do with religion. Hindu soldiers said that the grease was beef fat, and cows are sacred to Hindus. Muslims thought that it was pork fat, and Muslims are not allowed to eat pork.)

Indians called it a **rebellion** against foreign rule. They had a long list of complaints. The British had taken away the lands of the rajahs and nawabs. No Indians were employed as judges, army officers, or in other senior jobs. The British did not respect Indian customs and laws. And imports of British cotton cloth had damaged Indian trade.

The rebellion (or mutiny) failed. But the British learned lessons from it. They ended the rule of the East India Company. In future, a **viceroy** ruled India in the name of the queen. They went on using Indian troops, but the number of British soldiers in India was greatly increased.

Now try Exercises 15.1 and 15.2.

Source 15a

If I told you about all the things the rebels have done you would not believe me. Such awful crimes have never been known before. You in England will not hear the worst, for the worst is so bad that the papers would not dare publish it. The British soldiers here are furious. They say very little, but every face shows that when the time comes they will show no mercy to those who have shown none themselves.

Letter from a journalist in India to an English newspaper in 1857.

Exercise 15.1

Read **Section A**, then answer the questions. You can find the right answers, and some wrong ones, in the list below.
a   i Which words mean the same as 'rebellion'?
    ii Which words mean the same as 'mutiny'?
b According to the British, what was the main cause of the mutiny?
c According to Indians, what were the causes of the rebellion? (More than one answer.)

● The British brought law and order to India.
● A revolt by soldiers or sailors against their officers.
● The British did not understand or respect Indian ways.
● The viceroy ruled India in the name of the queen.
● Imported British goods harmed Indian trade.
● The British took land that belonged to Indian princes.
● A war against a foreign ruler.
● No Indians were employed in top jobs.
● Sepoys had to use greased cartridges.

Source 15b

It was a savage war. Both sides were guilty of dreadful crimes. At Cawnpore, Nana Sahib had all his British prisoners put to death. He did not even spare the women and children. But when the British took Delhi back, all the houses, shops, and stores were ransacked. The people in them were killed – men, women and children. Every British soldier became rich.

Adapted from a book written by D. P. Singhal, an Indian historian, in 1983.

Exercise 15.2

Read **Sources 15a** and **15b**. Then write out and complete the sentences.

a The author of **Source 15a** was shocked by _____ .
b **Source 15a** says that some of the crimes were so bad that _____ .
c **Source 15a** says that the British soldiers were _____ .
d **Source 15b** calls the mutiny a _____ .
e **Source 15b** says that the Indians murdered British _____ .
f **Source 15b** says that the British soldiers _____ .
g The two sources say different things because _____ .

The British brought industrial technology to India, e.g. by building railways. This is Victoria railway station in Bombay.

B The dominions

Britain did not treat her **white** subjects overseas in the same way as her black and Asian ones. The loss of the American colonies (see Chapter 2) taught her a lesson. She learned that it was wiser to share power with the colonists than to fight them. Before 1900, though, no-one in Britain thought that the same was true of subjects who were not white.

Canada was in two parts, one British and one French. Each of them got the right to govern itself in 1791. But after a revolt in 1837, the two parts were joined together. And an act passed in 1867 made Canada a **dominion**. This meant that it was almost free from British control. (The Queen of England was still Queen of Canada.)

Britain began sending convicts to **Australia** in 1787. But far more settlers went there of their own free will than in chains. Some went to look for gold, but most of them went as sheep-farmers. The wool they sent home kept the Yorkshire mills running. In 1850, there were 265,000 people in New South Wales, and **thirteen million** sheep!

The colonies in Australia got the right to govern themselves between 1856 and 1861. But it was not until the 1890s that they talked about joining together. In the end, they did so, and became a dominion, like Canada, in 1901. (**New Zealand** became a single state with the right to rule itself in 1876.)

Now try Exercise 15.3.

The British government took over from the East India Company as ruler of India after the Mutiny. In 1876, Parliament gave Queen Victoria the title 'Empress of India'.

Exercise 15.3

Read **Section B**. Draw a timeline from 1750 to 1901, and mark the following in the right places:

a Canada became a dominion.
b Australia became a dominion.
c New Zealand got the right to rule itself.
d The two parts of Canada got the right to govern themselves.
e The first settlement for convicts was set up in Australia.
f Revolt in Canada.
g Australian colonies got the right to elect their own governments.

C Empire-building

The trade in black slaves made some English merchants rich in the eighteenth century. But Parliament banned the slave trade in 1807. And in 1833 it ordered that the slaves should all be set free. In the **West Indies**, the freed slaves worked for wages on the sugar plantations. But the wages were low, partly because the price of sugar took a sharp fall.

The first white settlers at the **Cape of Good Hope** (see the **Map** below) were Dutch (or **Boers**). In 1815, the Cape became British. For the rest of the nineteenth century, there was a long string of quarrels between the British and the Boers. Britain lost the first **Boer War** in 1881. And the second Boer War (1899–1902) began badly as well.

The second half of the nineteenth century was a time of great growth in the British Empire. The reasons were mainly to do with trade. And trade with India and the Far East meant that the **Suez Canal**, which was built in 1869, was vital to Britain. So when there was disorder in **Egypt** in 1882, Britain used it as an excuse to send in troops and take over.

From the 1880s, a 'Scramble for Africa' took place, as the states of western Europe rushed to carve up the continent. They were all looking for new markets for the goods their industries produced. Soldiers came in with the traders, and the map of Africa was drawn to suit the statesmen of Europe. (Look at the **Map** below.)

Now try Exercise 15.4.

Africa in 1900

0   500   1000   1500 Km

N W E S

Atlantic Ocean

Indian Ocean

MOROCCO ALGERIA
LIBYA
Suez Canal
EGYPT
FRENCH WEST AFRICA
Red Sea
SUDAN
GOLD COAST
NIGERIA
LIBERIA
CAMEROON
ETHIOPIA
UGANDA
KENYA
CONGO
GERMAN EAST AFRICA
ANGOLA
RHODESIA
MOZAMBIQUE
MADAGASCAR
GERMAN SOUTH-WEST AFRICA
TRANS
O.F.S.
CAPE COLONY NATAL

British
French
Belgian
German
Portuguese

Italian
Spanish
Turkish
Independent

Boer republics at war with Britain 1899·1902:
TRANS = Transvaal
O.F.S. = Orange Free State

Troops leaving Southampton Dock to go and fight in the Boer War

Source 15c

At a time when people are demanding that our forces should attack Egypt, we have to ask the reason why. A few years ago, our government and the French began to interfere in Egypt, without having any right to do so. The result was that the National Party was formed. Its slogan was 'Egypt for the Egyptians'. If Englishmen cried 'England for the English' we would praise them. So why should we condemn Egyptians for doing the same?

Report of a meeting of the Workmen's Peace Association, 24 June 1882.

Source 15d

At last, the world has been taught what happens if England is defied and its subjects are killed. We regret the damage to Alexandria and its people. But in fact what has happened was good both for Egypt and for England. Egypt has been freed from the rule of the National Party tyrants. And the massacre of Englishmen has been avenged.

Amended from *The Observer* newspaper, 16 July 1882. (When Englishmen were killed in riots in Alexandria, the Royal Navy shelled the city.)

Explorers, such as David Livingstone, helped to spread the British Empire in Africa. This picture shows Livingstone on the River Shire in Malawi in 1859.

Exercise 15.4

Read **Section C** and **Sources 15c** and **15d**.
Write a short essay which answers these questions:

a What did the two sources think about the Egyptian National Party?
b What did the two sources think about using force against Egypt?
c Do you think that all British people were proud of the Empire? Do you think that they all had the same opinion?

16 Education

A Public schools and private schools

Source 16a

Most of the great 'public' schools of England took boarders and charged fees. They were for the **sons** of the rich, and were not **public** at all. They taught their pupils Latin and Greek, but not much mathematics, and no science, history, or French. Rich men's **daughters** stayed at home. They were taught by their mothers, or perhaps a governess.

Dissenters (Protestants who did not belong to the Church of England) had their own schools. They were the best in England. Only they taught science, commerce, French, and German. Many of the businessmen and inventors of the Industrial Revolution had been to dissenters' schools.

The very poor did not send their children to school, because they could not afford the fees. Also, they needed the wages that their children earned. But men and women who had just a little money sent their sons and daughters to **private** schools. Some of these were really awful. They had no proper books, desks, or classrooms, and the teachers were ignorant, greedy, and cruel.

Charities ran schools for the poor in some towns, but there were not enough of them. Then, in 1780, **Robert Raikes** opened his first **Sunday school** in Gloucester. His aim was to occupy the children of the poor, who worked in factories on week-days. (See **Source 16b**.) Some of the children learned to read and write. All of them were taught to obey 'their betters'.

Now try Exercises 16.1.

Farmer Giles and his wife show off their daughter, Betty, to their neighbours. Betty has just returned from a private school, where she has learned to play the piano and sing.

79

Source 16b

On Sundays the streets of Minchinhampton have always been full of half-naked, half-starved little brutes. But last Sunday I was pleased to see that the streets were empty. The children were all in the Sunday School. I found 300 of them there, all busy, some learning their letters, some learning to spell, and some reading the Bible. There was silence and good order, and all seemed happy and contented.

From the *Gloucester Journal* newspaper, 15 November 1784.

Exercise 16.1

Read **Section A** and **Source 16b**, and look at **Source 16a**.
Write four short paragraphs:

a What **facts** does **Source 16b** contain?

b What were the **opinions** of the author of **Source 16b**?

c Describe what you can see in **Source 16a**.

d In **Source 16a**, what do you think were the **opinions** of i Farmer Giles and his wife, ii Betty, iii Betty's younger sister, iv the neighbours, v the servant, vi the dog?

B Public money for schools

The biggest problem about schooling for the poor was money — the cost of teachers, books, etc. Soon after 1800, **Andrew Bell** and **Joseph Lancaster** found what seemed to be an answer. (See **Sources 16c** and **16d**.) They used **monitors**, and this was cheap — one person could teach a very large class.

Bell's and Lancaster's schools were run by societies which were linked to the Churches. And it was to these Church schools that the first grants of **public money** were made. In 1833, Parliament gave £20,000 to help with schooling for the poor. (Even in 1833, this was quite a small amount.)

The government gave more and more money to the Church schools during the next thirty years. By 1860, some people said that it was giving too much. So new rules, brought out in 1862, said that only schools which were doing a good job would get support. Inspectors went round, testing the pupils. Schools got so much for each pupil who passed the test. This was called '**payment by results**'.

Source 16c

By 1860, about half the children in England and Wales were getting some kind of schooling. But most of them left school before the age of twelve. Schools in Scotland were much better. And in many parts of Europe, education was **compulsory**.

People began to say that the state should take charge of schools in England and Wales as well. It should **force** parents to make their children attend. And state schools should be **free**. Some said that if the workers were not educated, British industry would fall behind its rivals. Others said that now that working men had the right to vote, they needed to be able to read and write. (See **Source 16g**.)

Now try Exercises 16.2 and 16.3.

Source **16d**

The cheapest way of teaching a large number of pupils is to use monitors. The teacher chooses the best pupils as monitors. He teaches them himself, then makes them pass on what they have learned to the rest of the pupils. In this way, the teacher gets a set of assistants, and does not need to pay them wages. Using this method, I have taught a class of 225 pupils.

Adapted from an article published in the *Quarterly Review* in 1831.

One of Joseph Lancaster's schools in the East End of London in 1839. The older boys acted as monitors, passing on knowledge to the younger boys. The toys hanging from the ceiling were given as rewards for good work and behaviour. The artist drew what he saw for himself, but we do not know his name.

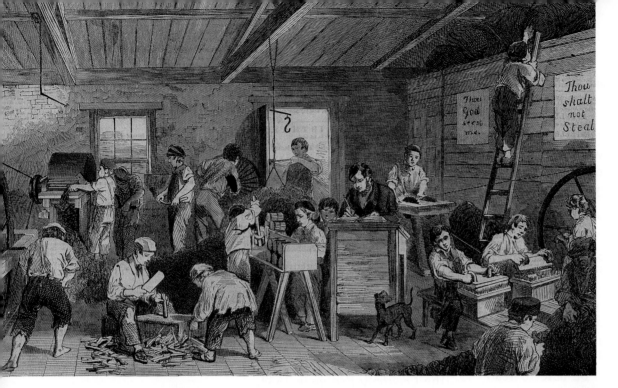

A 'ragged school' in 1853. This was a kind of charity school where poor children learned practical skills and moral values. The artist would have seen a ragged school, but his name is not known.

Source 16f

We know that there will always be some crime. But we should try to stop crime at its source. To do that we must teach children the difference between right and wrong, and make them learn God's laws. We must get them into the habit of obeying rules and orders. If we do that, when they become men they will obey the laws and keep order in our society.

From a speech made by Lord Palmerston, the Prime Minister, in 1860.

Source 16g

I suppose that we will now have to educate our masters. You have placed the government of this country in the hands of the masses. So you will now have to give them education. I used to be against education for all, but I am now ready to accept it.

Adapted from a speech made by Robert Lowe, M.P. in 1867, just after Parliament had given the vote to working men.

Exercise 16.2

Read **Section B** and **Sources 16d, 16f**, and **16g**. Look at **Sources 16c** and **16e**. Answer these questions about each of the sources:

a Who wrote or drew it? (Write 'not known' if you do not know.)
b When was it written or drawn?
c Is it a primary or a secondary source? (Look again at the note on page 32.)

Put your answers to questions **a, b,** and **c** above in a table, with columns for 'Source', 'Author or artist', 'Date', and 'Primary or secondary'.

Exercise 16.3

What were the **motives** of the authors of **Sources 16b, 16d, 16f**, and **16g**? — **Why** were they in favour of schools for the children of the working class? Discuss these questions in a group. Then make a group display:

a Write out the sources.
b Write paragraphs saying what the motives of the authors of the sources were.
c Draw cartoons to go with the written work.

Divide up these jobs among the members of the group.

C Board schools

An act passed in 1870 started a state system of schooling in England and Wales. But to save money, it did not go as far as many people would have liked. The act said that where there were church schools, they would continue to get public money. New schools would be built only where there were no church schools. The new schools would be called '**board schools**'.

The 1870 act did not make it **compulsory** to go to school. From 1880, though, parents were **compelled** to send children up to ten years old to school. By 1900, full-time schooling was compulsory up to the age of twelve. The 1870 act did not make education **free**, either. Parents had to pay nine old pence (about 4p.) a week for each child. (Board schools became free in 1891.)

Board schools, as a rule, were solid, dismal buildings, red brick outside and stone corridors and stairs inside. Iron railings round the concrete yards made them look even more like prisons. Most of them had no science labs, art or craft rooms, or gyms. P.E., which was called 'drill', was done outdoors, in the yard.

Classes were huge (sixty was common), and lessons were dull. The children were taught to read, write, and do simple sums, and they learned a lot of scripture. Sometimes, there was singing or drawing for a change. Boys and girls were shouted at for most of the time, and caned when they were slow to learn.

Now try Exercise 16.4.

Exercise 16.4

Read **Section C**. Copy the sentences and write TRUE or FALSE after each one.

a After 1870, Church schools got no more public money.

_____

b Board schools were built after the 1870 Education act.

_____

c After 1880, education was compulsory for children up to the age of ten. _____

d Parents still had to pay nine pence per week for each child at school in 1900. _____

e Board schools were made to look attractive to the pupils.

_____

f Most board schools had no playing fields. _____

g In board schools, classes were large and lessons were dull.

_____

h Boys could be caned in board schools, but girls could not.

_____

Boys' drill in a board school yard in around 1900

17 Arts and Leisure

Source 17a

A Architecture and painting

West Wycombe Park, a country house built in Buckinghamshire between 1735 and 1765 in the Roman and Greek style

Only the rich can afford to hire architects. And 'the rich' in the 1750s meant the landowners. They paid architects to design their country houses. And the architects of the time copied **Greek** and **Roman** styles, with columns and **grand doorways**. (Look at **Source 17a**.) Before long, the Greek and Roman style reached the towns as well. The finest streets and squares of Bath and London were built between 1760 and 1820. (Look at **Source 17b**.)

In the nineteenth century, though, big companies and town councils hired the architects. Some fine country houses were still being built. But the chief buildings of the years 1860 to 1900 were town halls and railway stations. At the same time, there was a change in style. The Greeks and Romans were out, and the **Middle Ages** were in. That is why St. Pancras Station in London looks like a cathedral. (Look at **Source 17d**.)

Source 17b

Regent Street in London as it was when first built in 1811

Source 17c

The Royal Pavilion in Brighton, designed for the Prince Regent (later King George IV) by his architect John Nash. It was completed in 1823. The design copies the palaces and temples of India.

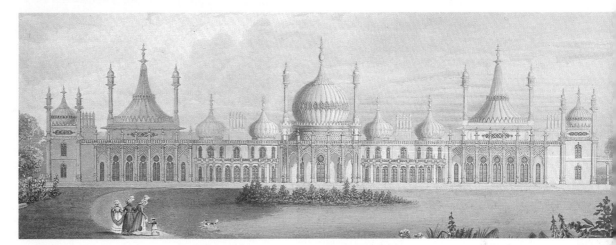

Source 17d

St. Pancras Station in London, which was built between 1868 and 1874

The great artists of the mid-eighteenth century painted **portraits**. By 1800, though, 'romantic' **landscapes** were much more popular. (Look at **Source 17e**.) Fifty years later, the public wanted pictures that told a **story**. So artists gave them scenes from history or the Bible, or views of modern craftsmen at work. (Look at **Source 17f**.)

Now try Exercise 17.1.

Source 17e

'Crossing the Brook', a landscape by J. M. W. Turner. The artist lived from 1775 to 1851.

Source 17f

'Iron and Coal', painted by William Bell Scott in 1861

Exercise 17.1

Read **Section A**. Look at **Sources 17a**, **17b**, **17c**, **17d**, **17e**, and **17f**. Draw a timeline from 1750 to 1900. Mark on it 'mid-eighteenth century', 'late eighteenth century', 'early nineteenth century', etc.
Mark the following at the right points on the time line:

a West Wycombe Park was completed.
b Regent Street was built.
c The Royal Pavilion, Brighton was completed.
d St. Pancras Station was completed.
e J. M. W. Turner was born.
f W. B. Scott painted 'Iron and Coal'.

B Fashion

In clothes, also, fashions were set by the rich. They could afford a lot of new clothes, and could keep up with the changing styles. Fashion did not mean much to the poor, except when they could get hold of rich men's and women's cast-offs. For that reason, poor people's fashions were a few years behind the styles of the rich.

Women's dresses were always long, but their shape changed. Hooped petticoats in the mid-eighteenth century gave way to the straight 'Empire line' of 1800. (Look at **Sources 17g** and **17h**.) By the 1850s, metal supports were back with the 'crinoline'. And this in turn was replaced by the 'bustle' in the 1870s. (Look at **Sources 17i** and **17j**.)

Between 1750 and 1900, men's fashions changed much more than women's. They stopped wearing wigs before 1800. By the mid-nineteenth century, they were wearing **trousers**, not breeches. And **suits**, not very different from those that are worn today, had appeared by the 1880s. All this time, men's clothes had been growing less colourful – no men dressed in pale blue or yellow by 1900.

Now try Exercise 17.2.

Source 17g

Fashionable dress in the 1760s. The man wears a silk, embroidered coat, a flowered silk waistcoat, knee breeches, and white stockings. The woman wears a cream satin gown with a hooped skirt. Both wear powdered wigs.

Source 17h

Fashion in 1800. The woman wears an 'Empire line' gown in the Greek style, with no hoops and only one petticoat. The man still wears knee breeches, but the coat is cut in a different style, and he has a 'Beaver' top hat, and black leather boots.

Source 17i

Fashion in the 1850s. The man wears a black silk top hat, a frock coat, and trousers. The woman wears a ball dress of white crinoline with a taffeta bodice and overskirt.

Source 17j

A lady of the 1870s. She wears a dark brown silk afternoon dress with a bustle skirt.

Source 17k

Men's fashion in the 1880s. He wears a brown tweed suit and a black bowler hat.

Women's tennis outfit in the 1890s. She plays tennis in a striped blouse, a long serge skirt, a black belt and tie, with black canvas shoes, and a straw hat.

Exercise 17.2

Read **Section B**. Look at **Sources 17g, 17h, 17i, 17j,** and **17k**. Write a short essay, describing

either a the changes in women's fashion between 1750 and 1880,

or b the changes in men's fashion between 1750 and 1880.

Draw at least one picture to go with your essay.

C Sport and entertainment

To the upper classes, 'sport' meant killing birds and animals — **shooting** and **fox-hunting**. The landlord's hounds could chase the fox through his tenant's crops. And no-one but the landlord could take his 'game'. The laws against **poaching** were severe.

Many a young man 'of good family' lost his money and land gambling on cards, dice, or horses. After 1800, though, **racing** became more honest and fair. It also became a sport for all classes, not just the rich. After 1850, a trip to Epsom on Derby Day was a treat for thousands of London families.

In 1750, **cricket** was a game played on the village green. **Football** was more like a war between rival sides. The nineteenth century saw both games turned into formal sports, with fixed rules. By the 1890s, large crowds were turning out to watch professional players in cup-ties and test-matches. **Lawn-tennis**, on the other hand, was a

new sport. It was invented in the 1870s as a pastime for people with big houses and gardens.

The **theatre** was popular in London in 1750. Soon after 1800, most of the large towns outside London had theatres too. But the theatre was for people with some money. After 1850, the middle class went to the **music-hall**, where they could drink, watch the acts, and join in the songs. For working-class men, and some women, there was the **public house**.

Before 1850, working people did not take **holidays**. But the railways made travel quick and cheap. And the rising standard of living meant that there was more money to spend. So some people could take day-trips to the seaside. And by 1900, more and more could look forward to a week each year at Blackpool or Margate.

Now try Exercises 17.3 and 17.4.

An F.A. Cup tie between Notts County and Blackburn Rovers in 1891

Exercise I7.3

Read **Section C**, and look at the illustrations connected with sport. Write notes (in your own words) on the following:

a The favourite sports of the gentry.
b The changes in football and cricket.
c Sporting clothes in the 1890s.
d Theatres and music-halls.
e Holidays

Source 17l

A street musician in 1877

Source 17m

> To many people, street music is a great nuisance, but there are far more who enjoy it. The upper class can afford to go to the opera and the best concerts. The middle class and the tradesmen have their music halls. But the working class can not afford even the music halls. The street bands and organs are their entertainment. The noise they make is sometimes awful, but a big crowd gathers whenever a band begins to play.

Adapted from *The Observer* newspaper, 3 July 1864.

Exercise I7.4

Read **Source 17m** and look at **Source 17l**.
Then fill in the blank spaces in the sentences.

a The people who objected to music in the street could probably afford to go to the _____ or _____ hall.
b Working-class people must have liked street bands, because big _____ gathered to listen to them.
c The words 'there are far more who enjoy it' in **Source 17m** tell us that the _____ class must have been bigger than the other classes.
d Opera and concert tickets must have been _____ in the 1860s.
e Music halls must have been _____ expensive than the opera house.
f The street musician in **Source 17l** is playing a _____ .
g **Sources 17l** and **17m** both say that people _____ street music in working-class districts.

18 Religion

A The Church of England

In 1750, the great majority of people in Britain were Christians. And well over half of those in England and Wales belonged to the **Church of England**. But the Church of England was more suited to the past than to the future.

Each village or group of villages formed a **parish**. And each parish had its church and parson. With the Industrial Revolution, some villages grew into towns. But still there was one parish church, and one parson. In the new towns, there was often no church near to where the people lived. And there was no parson to visit them when they needed help or comfort.

Some parsons worked very hard. But too many, especially in the country districts, took life easily. They were more keen to be on good terms with the local gentry than working among the poor. The **bishops** should have given them a lead. But too many bishops were more bothered about their own careers than the clergy they should have led and guided.

One group within the Church of England saw that all was not well. The **evangelicals** were keen to preach the Christian message in the new towns. They wanted people to read the Bible for themselves, so they were in favour of schools for the poor. But they were shocked by what they saw in the factories and mills. This is what led them to press for changes in the law. (See **Section C**.)

Now try Exercise 18.1.

Source 18a

Churches were often full on Sundays in the mid-eighteenth century, even if some of the congregation fell asleep!

Source 18b

The bishops are worried about a planned inquiry into their incomes. They are afraid that the government might take some of their money away.

John Wesley preaching from his father's tomb

B The Methodists

John Wesley was a Church of England parson and a great preacher. Crowds flocked to hear him as he travelled round the country. Between 1738 and 1791, it is reckoned that he travelled 224,000 miles on horseback, and preached 40,000 sermons. The men and women who followed his lead were called '**Methodists**'.

Wesley said that he had been 'converted' suddenly, one day in May 1738. In a flash, he had seen that God loved him, and that he was 'saved'. He spent the rest of his life – another 53 years – touring England and Wales, begging people to let God 'save' them too.

In a lot of places, Wesley was not allowed to preach in the church. In a good many places, there was no church to preach in. So he did a great deal of his preaching in the open air. This suited him well – he could reach a bigger audience that way. Men and women came to his meetings in thousands. And they did not just listen in silence — they sang, cried out, wept, danced, and jumped for joy.

Wesley and other Methodist preachers won a huge following, mainly among working people, both in the towns and on the land. By 1791, there were over a million Methodists. In one important sense, though, Wesley failed. He wanted Methodists to remain in the Church of England. But soon after his death, the Methodists and the Church of England split apart for good.

Now try Exercise 18.2.

William Wilberforce

Source **18c**

Joseph Rawlins, who was known as the 'pit preacher', died not long ago in Staffordshire. He got his nickname because he acted for many years as a Methodist minister for the miners in those parts. He first became a Methodist after he heard John Wesley preach in 1749. Rawlins was blind, but he worked on week-days as a miner. He gave most of his wages away to the sick and the poor.

From the *Bristol Journal* newspaper, 11 June 1791.

Exercise 18.2

Read **Section B** and **Source 18c**. Which of the statements below do you think is true? Write out the sentences which you think are true.

a All Methodist ministers were Church of England parsons.
b John Wesley preached in Staffordshire in 1749.
c Most Church of England parsons did not approve of John Wesley.
d A lot of miners in Staffordshire were Methodists.
e Joseph Rawlins died in 1793.
f Some Methodist ministers had week-day jobs as well as preaching on Sundays.
g John Wesley would have been sad if he had known that the Methodists left the Church of England.
h Working people had no interest in religion.
i Methodists believed in giving money to the sick and poor.

C The Churches and reform

Between 1750 and 1900, trade and industry made Britain rich and strong. She became the 'workshop of the world', she gained a great empire, and her navy ruled the seas. But there was a dark side to all this success. This was the suffering of the black slaves and the children in the mills. It was the women in the mines and the crowded families in the filthy slums.

Evangelicals, such as **William Wilberforce**, tried to put right these wrongs. Wilberforce spent his life

fighting for the rights of slaves. In 1807, he and his friends got Parliament to ban the **trade** in slaves. But it was not until 1833, the year of his death, that all the slaves in the British Empire were freed.

Lord Shaftesbury was troubled by the 'slaves' in the mills and mines. He was the leader of the 'Ten Hours Movement'. This was a group of evangelicals in Parliament, who wanted to shorten the working day to no more than ten hours. They had some success

— Factory Acts passed in the 1830s and 1840s cut children's hours of work and banned women from the mines. In the end, they led to shorter hours for men as well.

After 1870, reformers turned to **housing** for the poor. **Cardinal Manning**, the leading Catholic, tried to improve the state of London's slums. Some charities put up new blocks of flats. But the best work in this field was done by **George Cadbury**, a Quaker, and the head of a chocolate firm. At Bournville, near Birmingham, he housed his workers in a brand new town.

Now try Exercises 18.3 and 18.4.

Exercise 18.3

Read **Section C**. Find words or phrases in **Section C** which mean the same as the following:

a Black workers who were owned by their employers. _____

b Dirty, overcrowded, badly-built housing. _____

c Members of the Church of England who were in favour of reform. _____

d M.P.s who wanted to cut the working day. _____

e A new law to do with hours and conditions in factories. _____

f Organizations which collect money and try to help those in need. _____

g A new town for workers in a chocolate factory. _____

Lord Shaftesbury inspecting conditions in a coal mine

Source 18d

Pass through Edinburgh on a Sunday morning and you will not meet a soul. The streets are silent and empty. But the moment prayers are over, they pour out of the churches in crowds. After spending some time at home, they go back to church again. But at five o-clock prayers are over for the day, and they begin to amuse themselves. The young ones go for walks in the meadows. The older folks meet in groups to discuss the scandal of the town.

Adapted from a book written by Captain Topham in 1776. The Scots people belonged to the Church of Scotland, which was different from the Church of England. It had no bishops, the minister did not read the service from a prayer book, and the sermons were longer.

Source 18e

In Birmingham there is one fine large church. There are also three chapels and eight meeting houses for Dissenters. But the great mass of people do not care about religion. They seldom, if ever, go to church, and spend Sundays in their working clothes, amusing themselves.

Adapted from W. Thompson's *A Tour of England and Scotland*, written in 1788. The 'fine large church' would belong to the Church of England. 'Dissenters' were Protestants who did not belong to the Church of England. Methodists would count as 'Dissenters'.

Exercise 18.4

Read **Sources 18d** and **18e** and the notes which go with them.
Write an essay with the title 'Sunday in Edinburgh and Birmingham'. Your essay should answer these questions:

a Who wrote these sources? Which source was written first? How many years were there between them?
b How were Sundays different in Edinburgh and Birmingham?
c Which Church did the people of Edinburgh belong to?
d Were the people of Edinburgh all devout Christians?
e What kind of churches were there in Birmingham?
f Can you think of any reasons why most people in Birmingham did not go to church?

Sunday in Edinburgh, according to Source 18d

Sunday in Birmingham, according to Source 18e

Cross references between exercises and the revised National Curriculum Programme of Study

(Those printed in bold type are particularly relevant)

Chronological understanding

Chapters	1	2	3	4	5	6	7	8	9	10	11	12	13	14	15	16	17	18
a Historical knowledge	1.1 1.3	2.1	3.1 3.4	4.1	5.2	6.4	7.1	8.1	9.1	10.3 10.4	11.1	12.1	13.3	14.1	15.1 15.4	16.4	17.1 17.3	18.1
b Concepts and terminology	1.5				5.5			8.5						14.4				18.3
c Chronology dates and sequence		2.2				6.4				10.3			13.3		15.3		17.1	
d Chronology – conventions				**4.1**	5.3				9.1								17.1	

Knowledge and understanding

	1	2	3	4	5	6	7	8	9	10	11	12	13	14	15	16	17	18
a Cause and consequence			**3.4**				7.5					12.3			15.1			
b Motivation					**5.2**			8.2			11.4		13.1			16.3		
c Continuity and change			3.1	4.2					9.4			12.2					17.2	
d Different features of situations	1.2					6.1	**7.3**							14.2	15.4			

Historical interpretation

	1	2	3	4	5	6	7	8	9	10	11	12	13	14	15	16	17	18
a Distinguishing fact and fiction				4.3				**8.3**		10.4								
b Different versions of events and topics		2.3			5.4	6.3												18.4
c Recognizing fact and opinion	**1.4**						7.4					12.4		14.3		16.1		
d Different interpretations			3.3						9.2		**11.3**		13.4		15.2			
e Reasons for different interpretations		**2.3**			5.4	6.3									15.2			18.4

Historical enquiry

	1	2	3	4	5	6	7	8	9	10	11	12	13	14	15	16	17	18
a Acquiring information	1.3		3.2				7.4	8.4		10.4							17.3	18.2
b Sources – authorship and dates				4.3				8.3			11.2					16.2		
c Primary and secondary sources						**6.2**		8.4			11.2					16.2		
d Making deductions from sources			3.2				7.2			**10.2**		12.4					17.4	18.2
e Using different kinds of source		2.4			5.1		7.2		9.3					14.3		16.1		
f Value and reliability of evidence				4.4					**9.3**	10.1			13.2					

Most of the exercises also seek to develop organisation and communication skills.